Romantic At-Home Dinners

Sneaky Strategies for Couples with Kids

NAN BOOTH
GARY FISCHLER

BRIGHTON PUBLICATIONS, INC.

Copyright © Nan Booth

Brighton Publications, Inc.
P.O. Box 120706
St. Paul, MN 55112-2220
(612-636-2220

First Edition: 1994

Library of Congress Cataloging-in-Publication Data
Booth, Nan
    Romantic at-home dinners : sneaky strategies for couples with kids / Nan Booth, Gary Fischler. — 1st ed.
        p. cm.
    Includes index.
        1. Cookery. 2. Cookery for two. 3. Menus.   I. Fischler, Gary, II Title.
TX652.B66 1994   93-33634
641.5'6 — dc20   CIP
            ISBN 0-918420-19-9

Printed in the United States of America

To

Jacob and Nathan

ACKNOWLEDGEMENTS

One is never alone in a project like this, and we owe thanks to many people. Unfortunately, we can't thank all of the past generations of fine parents and creative cooks who made us what we are today. And we don't see how we could list all of the people with whom we have cooked, dined, exchanged recipes, exulted and commiserated about parenthood, and generally discussed the finer things in life over the years, but they know who they are.

We can thank Susan Perry, Laurie Schmidt, and Amy Frankfurt, who were all instrumental in formulating and clarifying the idea for the book, and Gary Schoener, who provided support and advice.

Mary Rathke told us about roasting garlic, for which we will be eternally grateful. Michelle Magnani gave us her Caesar Salad recipe, Margaret Schneider her Green Salad with Strawberries and Poppy Seed Dressing, and Rosemary Booth her Lemon Souffle, which some of us remember from childhood.

Jeff Comins contributed his delicious version of Long Island Ice Tea, and Fred Booth his Manhattan, which is in the running for Most Perfect Cocktail Ever Created. Steven Westby's expertise and enthusiasm on the subject of wine helped us immeasurably, not only in our work on this book, but also in the quality of our lives. Steven is the Wine Manager at Surdyks Liquor Store, in Minneapolis.

Barb Strand gave us the benefit of her experience working on numerous cookbooks; she helped with the format and phrasing of our recipes.

Last, but certainly not least, are those who tirelessly and enthusiastically tested our recipes: Carolyn Halliday and Dorothy Edelson.

TABLE OF CONTENTS

Contents

Macaroni and Cheese (With Hamburgers on Buns) / Green Noodles and Ham (With Apologies to Dr. Seuss)

5 OH BOY, BEDTIME! / 44

Even very young children are capable of understanding that parents sometimes need "grown-up" time. Learn how to plan activities to keep children of all ages occupied so you can be alone, including how to make an early bedtime seem really fun.

Who's in Charge? / The Family Schedule / Acclimate Baby / Adjust Toddler's Schedule / Bribe-Taking: Ages Three to Six / Independent: Ages Six to Nine / Almost Grown-up: Ages Nine to Twelve / See, It Worked

6 HERE WE ARE, WHAT DO WE TALK ABOUT? / 52

If you remember the romance of your pre-child evenings together, you will also remember that you hardly ever talked about toilet training or Little League car pools. Learn how to talk to each other again. Learn how to deepen intimacy, how to increase your appreciation for each other, and how to use conversation to rekindle romance.

Learning to Talk / The "I-Statement" / Open Ended Questions / Specialty Tools / Sweet Memories / Shared Dreams / Planning the Future / Live in the Present / The Rules

7 IN THE SPIRIT OF THE EVENING: COCKTAILS AND WINE / 60

Cocktails and wine can enhance your romantic evening at home. Here, the subject is sufficiently de-mystified so that you will be able to mix great cocktails and stop being intimidated by wine merchants. You will be the new expert.

Enjoy Moderation / Cocktails / Bourbon Drinks / Gin and Rum / Wine / Wine in Winter / Springtime Wine / High Summer Wines / Autumn Wine / Toasting

8 JUST DESSERTS AND OTHER DELIGHTS / 69

You need not undertake the entire production of a romantic dinner at home to achieve the desired effect. Remember that part of a romantic dinner is better than none, especially if it's the dessert part, with cappuccino, in front of the fire. In fact, you don't have to eat at all; there are plenty of ways to find romantic time together at home, after the kids go to bed.

Contents

Contents

Chapter
1

Part one:

GETTING ROMANTIC

THE ROMANTIC DINNER IDEA

*O*ne evening, after the kids were in bed, we began to reminisce about calamari. Delicate in flavor, crispy in texture, a bit exotic, calamari dipped in a tangy sauce represented unsurpassed dining pleasure. But we didn't stop there. Calamari was only the appetizer. We teased and tantalized each other with images of fresh pasta, elegant sauces, succulent shellfish, warm crusty bread, chocolate cheesecake, and so on, until our mouths watered and we begged each other for mercy.

Food was not the real topic of our conversation, though. We were really talking about romance — small candlelit cafes, our eyes meeting across the table, savoring our meal as we savored each other. Our nostalgia was for a different time in our lives, a time only for each other, a time before we knew anything at all about diapers, two o'clock feedings, chicken pox, baby sitters, dance classes, training wheels, macaroni and cheese, Nintendo, or coaching T-ball. Parenthood was certainly everything we thought it would be, and more.

We realized that we hadn't seen the inside of a small candlelit cafe in some time, and had instead begun to frequent the kinds of places that involve standing in line and don't serve calamari. This led us to other sobering realizations about our relationship. Not only did we miss calamari, we missed each other. We missed good conversation. We missed the kind of time together that keeps marriage fun, that keeps romance alive, and that makes it possible to sit through preschool music programs.

Not that we hadn't tried going out. The first time, the baby sitter called just as our hors d'oeuvre was served to say that our child had not stopped crying since we left, which seriously compromised our enjoyment of the meal. Another time, we made the mistake of calculating how many diapers we could have bought with the tip we left. But the worst was the time the sitter canceled on our anniversary, when we were all dressed up and ready to go to a restaurant that required reservations three weeks in advance. We were a bit discouraged.

So, a few nights after our conversation, when the kids were in bed, we laid out a red checkered tablecloth, lit a candle in an old chianti bottle, poured a little brandy into snifters, and sank our teeth into a frozen cheese-cake, which we had the foresight to thaw ahead of time. We held hands in the candlelight, put forkfuls of cheesecake into each other's mouths, and talked of love. We may even have talked of sex. In any case, we woke up the next morning feeling a lot like we used to feel after our first nights together. We didn't even mind much that it was six o'clock and the toddler standing beside our bed was in need of an immediate diaper change. We were renewed; we could handle it.

FINDING DINNER SUPPLIES

That was only the beginning. We located a source of fresh seafood in our land-locked city, learned to cook calamari the way we liked it and then lots of ways we didn't know we liked, discovered how yeast works (very well), bought a hand pasta machine, and experimented with chocolate in its various forms and permutations. We became expert planners, shoppers, kitchen innovators, and suppliers of romantic atmosphere, all against a backdrop of scraped knees and runny noses.

We no longer had any difficulty figuring out what to give each other on birthdays, Valentine's Day, Mother's Day, Father's Day, anniversaries, and so on; we bought candle holders, flower vases and compact discs. We bought matched sets of two in everything from champagne flutes to embroidered pillowcases, with a sense of purpose unknown when we had looked at the same kinds of things as wedding gifts. This was different; the object wasn't a public ceremony, but a secret tryst. Each gift became a token of our commitment to have more fun together. And we were delighted to find a place in our lives for those intriguing garments that you see in lounge wear catalogues but can't imagine yourself wearing.

We found something much more important, though, beyond food and beyond things. We remembered why we got married in the first place. It had a lot more to do with liking each other's company than with any desire to dazzle each other with our ability to locate stuffed animals under a crib in the dark. We knew that our children deserved all the available love, warmth, and nurturing in our household, and that there was plenty to go around, as long as the supply could be renewed. We figured out how to renew the supply.

RELATIONSHIP WORK

The injunction to couples that they must "work" on their relationship seems an unfortunate choice of words. You can work on painting your house, folding laundry, or building a bookcase. You can work on learning the oboe, mastering the stock market, or knitting a sweater. You can work on your golf swing. You can even work on your job. But how do you work on something that involves another autonomous and unpredictable person, the one in whose hands you chose to place your future marital happiness? Better to play together, and that is at least half of what relationship work is.

The other half has to do with how you play together. We all do better in an atmosphere of respect for our abilities and encouragement to try new things, and it's a lot more fun if we can talk with each other about our hopes, fears, failures, and successes as we go along

Regardless of the phrasing, the fact remains that in order to thrive, a marriage, like any other living thing, needs time and attention, nurturing and care. So do children; they're living things, too. In fact, parents spend their entire adult lives, at least until they retire and the kids move out, tossed about in the treacherous waters of things, living and otherwise, that require work, time, attention, nurturing, and care. The ability to set priorities becomes a survival skill.

Those waters are even more treacherous alone, so the first priority is each other. The goal is to create a loving, fun, and private place in an open boat on the high seas, when your crew is hungry and you are pursued by pirates. In other words, you must find the time for a love life without neglecting the children or breaking the budget. The real danger is that if the goal isn't accomplished, you're still out there, with no way to replenish your supplies.

Children need so much that it's easy to forget that you need stuff, too. You need grown-up stuff. Some of it you get from friends, some from a sense of accomplishment and purpose at work, some from finally achieving a respectable backhand. But some you can only get from each other, because you're not married to anyone else. Far from diminishing your capacity to meet your children's needs, meeting your own is your only hope. In fact, it's part of your job.

Your primary relationship is still with each other, though it often seems as though paying the bills and feeding the baby take precedence. And certainly, in order to accomplish the countless little daily tasks, let alone the major lifetime works, you need to be able to take each other for granted a little bit. You have to trust each other to stick it out. It all started with just the two of you, and, presumably, that's the way you want it to end, so you need all the tools you can get. Your supply list includes large amounts of tolerance, an ability to keep your mouth shut, and a certain blindness born of acceptance.

You can grit your teeth, pull your coat collar up around your ears, and head directly into the storm, hoping you'll both land on the other side with some of your feelings for each other intact, or you can put in to port whenever possible for R and R.

ROMANCE?

If you elect to try the latter approach, remember that grown-up fun includes romance. If your idea of a good time with each other is shooting a game of cut-throat pool down at your corner bar, or hanging out at the library seeing who can come up with the most references to Wordsworth's opinion of pleasure, or watching old *Star Trek* reruns, terrific, don't stop. And if, through the mysterious workings of passion, these activities have the effect of enhancing your love life, so much the better. That is part of the purpose of romance.

But there is more to it. Romance is less about what you do and more about how you do it. It's about your approach to life. For our purposes, it's about your approach to married life. Even more to the point, it's about your approach to married life once you have become mired in the joys of parenthood. It's an approach that looks for the special part, the fun part, the adventure, finds some of it every day, and finds a way to express it. If you are reading this amid the sounds of a raging battle over whose turn it is to choose which Nintendo game to play, the quest for a romantic life may seem as heroic and remote as the feats of chivalry performed by the medieval knights who inspired the term.

Nevertheless, it is your duty to each other and to your children to take it on. Why? Because like fine art, music, and literature, like a good movie, like a garden full of peonies, or a cold beer on a hot day, it makes life better. With it, a trip to the grocery store together is a thrill; without it, a moonlight walk by the sea is a yawn.

FOOD AND LOVE

All of which brings us back to food. Pretty much anything brings us back to food. Your three squares a day can be just another example of humdrum drudgery, or they can be occasions for celebration and joy. Not that you have to prepare gourmet meals all the time — macaroni and cheese exists for a reason. It's your approach to mealtime that counts. Of all the things that have to be done on a daily basis, only eating lends itself to such constant, far reaching, and varied opportunities for delight.

And eating together has long provided lovers with opportunities for nurturing romance. Whether it's the knight slaying the hart for his lady love's feast, or you sharing a truffle at the chocolate shop at the mall, food and love are a natural fit.

Food is sensuous. It is an aesthetic pleasure, both to the palate and to the eye. Picture Cezanne's apples, for instance, or a bakery showcase, or a bright red bowl overflowing with fluffy white popcorn. Even our edition of *Joy of Cooking* compares ratatouille to a Braque still life. Food also gratifies the physical appetites, and thus satisfies sensual needs unlike anything except sex, which is why so many dates involve going out to dinner. Remember the eating scene in the movie *Tom Jones*?

Food is a gift. Maybe your mother made your favorite meal on your birthday (fried chicken and mashed potatoes, was it? or hot dogs and baked beans? or linguini with mussels and anchovies?), or maybe you just wished she would. In any case, identifying and providing favorite foods for each other is a time honored expression of love. Knowing the perfect degree of doneness for your lover's steak, knowing that your lover actively seeks out opportunities to use mustard, or understanding a fondness for kasha knishes, creates a degree of intimacy and a depth of gratitude that is hard to match.

Food is an expression of individuality, a source of creativity. Exploring uncharted gastronomic territory, sharing discoveries and adventures, breaking new ground, and laying claim to new favorites known only to the two of you, has a way of forging unbreakable emotional bonds.

THE WAY IT WAS

Think back to your first date. Did you go out to dinner? Did you stop for cheesecake and cappuccino after the concert? Or maybe you just shared a box of Junior Mints at the movie. Whatever it was, food probably played a role. It might have been wonderful, exceptional food, or very ordinary food that was transformed by being part of your first date. Maybe you celebrated your one month anniversary by going out to dinner. Surely you took each other out to dinner to celebrate birthdays. Where did you go? What did you eat? What were your favorites? What places did you discover, where no one else had ever been?

Soon, you were going out to dinner on a regular basis, trying new places just for the fun of it, and at some point you started inviting each other to dinner at your respective apartments. If you are not sure how romantic that was, check Thomas Wolfe's *The Web and the Rock* out of your library, and read the passages that describe George and Esther's meals together. Read them out loud to each other, in bed.

By the time you were having breakfast together, you knew a lot about how to turn each other on, gastronomically speaking. If you think about it, you will probably realize that eating together had a lot to do with the romance in your relationship.

Now, as you try to peel carrots while holding the baby, dish out portions of Tater Tots before rushing off to Karate class, and sweep peas off the floor, the connection may seem tenuous. Trying to convince a preschooler that most people who eat spaghetti eat sauce with it can take the fun out of supper time. Cleaning rice florentine out of a toddler's hair can ruin your appetite. Listening to complaints about your innovations ("not stir-fry again") can squash your creativity. Mealtime with children is more of an exercise in damage control than an opportunity for romance and adventure.

ROMANCE AT HOME

Luckily, there is a solution. You'll be relieved to know that the romance in your relationship isn't dead, it's just wounded. It can be revived with a little care and attention. Likewise, you have not enjoyed your last quiet little supper of shrimp scampi or mustard-herb duck, free of spilled milk and your children's idea of dinner table conversation ("Daddy, where do boogers come from?" began one of ours).

As soon as we identified the serious romance gap in our relationship, we realized that the solution was at home. It's true that a solution anyplace else was out of the question at the time. We could barely afford the places that involve standing in line, let alone the restaurants we remembered or the hotel rooms we dreamed of.

It's also true that we are the sort of people who find the solution to most problems at home. We were on the vanguard of the "cocooning" trend, finding not only peace and solace, but also fun and adventure at home. We both work at home; even a ten minute commute seems too tedious. We may have the largest private library of video tapes in the Western World because we can't be bothered going out to movies. In general, we think that home is about the most appealing place on the planet.

Still, even for those couples who normally seek their fun, adventure and romance out in the big world, bringing it all back home adds a fascinating new dimension.

Make your home into a very private candlelit cafe. You not only have your own menu, tailored to your own highly individualized tastes, you also have your own music, your own flowers, your own carefully chosen dinner plates, cappuccino cups, and brandy snifters, and, just down the hall, your own bedroom. And you're already wearing "something more comfortable."

It's not hard to do. Really. What do you do with the children? See Chapter Five. How do you go about planning such an event? See Chapter Two. You think that the toddler sized slide and climber in your living room detracts from the romantic atmosphere? Turn the lights down lower. Or, make a trip to your local antique store and spend a few bucks on a romantic looking old throw or quilt or bedspread, and cover the pile of bright colored plastic for the evening.

You've never cooked anything more complicated than Shake n' Bake chicken and you don't think you can? Relax; though many would have us believe otherwise, there's no mystery to cooking. If you can read, you can cook. If you are motivated by a desire to experience the world's most succulent flavors on your tongue, you can learn to cook very well. If you are a person who connects food and love, the creations of the greatest chefs will not surpass yours. If your sense of adventure and your willingness to take a little risk extends from your cooking to your love life, your marriage will flourish, too.

DECISION TIME

So, if you are people who like to eat, who miss romantic time with each other, and who are at all comfortable in the kitchen, it's time to take charge. Make a decision. Think it over, though. If either of you has a strong aversion to some aspect of life in the kitchen, the clean-up aspect, for example, you will need to find another method of renewing your relationship; Chapter Eight contains some suggestions.

Once you decide to embark on this sensual quest for the pleasures of the palate and renewed marital bliss, toast your commitment with a glass of champagne, and make some plans. Even before you had children, when you prided yourselves on your spontaneity, you had to do some planning. You may not have minded waiting around in the lounge for the restaurant to seat you without a reservation, but if you wanted to go to a concert or a movie, too, you had to stick to a schedule. It was a lot easier in those days, though. With children in the picture, planning ahead is not only essential, it is a multi-faceted, many dimensional task that requires superior organizational skills. Planning to have your fun at home is often a lesser challenge than planning to go out.

Once you make the effort, and put the structure in place, you will be amazed at how easy it is, and how well it works. If eating together increases intimacy, so does working together. That's the whole idea behind creating a home and family in the first place.

Develop a romantic outlook on life. Look for the fun. Find the humor. Didn't you used to find your sweetheart's annoying habit of indecisiveness endearing? Didn't you used to laugh over that inexplicable inability to keep track of time?

Romance is about the daily things — a smile, a touch, a wink, a private joke, a cocktail before supper. Toast each other. Call each other pet names. Kiss each other hello and good-bye.

Romance is about adventure. You don't know each other as well as you think you do, and you never will. This gives your relationship a sense of mystery and intrigue that you don't want to lose. Keep the element of surprise, and use it.

On the other hand, you also know each other better than you think you do. Make the most of it. Listen carefully to each other. No one else has the ability to give to either of you what you can give to each other.

Use this book as a starting place. Don't think of it as a prescription, but as an idea bank. Adapt it to your own needs, tastes and circumstances. Adapt the recipes in Part Two to your own palate and skill level. Make up your own. Unleash your creativity. Bon voyage. Even though your adventures will take place in the privacy of your own home, you'll find an itinerary and some maps in the next chapter.

Chapter 2

PLANNING YOUR ROMANTIC EVENING

*R*oll up your sleeves. Sharpen your pencils. The Romance Committee has some work to do. Of course, figuring out how to have a good time is not unpleasant work.

As any committee veteran can tell you, the first step in planning is what the charming language of bureaucracy calls a "needs assessment." What do you have, what do you need, where can you get it, and how much will it cost?

In the language of love, your starting place is pretty much the same. What romantic capabilities does your home have? A fireplace, a porch, a bay window? A sauna and jacuzzi? That ridiculously ornate candelabra that Aunt Ruby gave you for a wedding gift? What essentials are you missing? Still using old mayonnaise jars for flower vases? What does your neighborhood have in the way of kitchen supply stores, antique stores, liquor stores, grocery stores, or delicatessens? What can you afford?

BUDGET BUYS

In consideration of that last point, keep two things in mind. First, many wonderful little artifacts, things like candle holders, flower vases, dessert plates, and embroidered throw pillows, can be bought for a song or less at a second-hand store. You don't need the Waterford crystal to achieve the desired effect. By the same token, hardware stores or discount stores are often excellent sources of kitchen equipment, at prices likely to be considerably less than those charged by your local gourmet shop.

On the other hand, when you consider the savings in doing all this at home instead of going out to an expensive restaurant and paying a baby sitter, new financial vistas open up. Invest in a cappuccino maker, for example, for about what a dinner at a nice restaurant would cost, and enjoy cappuccino whenever you want it for years to come. Think of it this way: you can buy an awful lot of fresh seafood to cook at home for what it would cost to eat bouillabaisse in a fancy restaurant downtown.

FOOD SOURCES

Which brings up another point to consider in your planning. How easy is it to get fresh seafood, or fresh pasta, or fresh strawberries, or saffron or morels or wild rice, in your neighborhood? If it isn't easy, is it possible? If it isn't possible, do you have other options? If not, then your menus will depend on the ingredients that you can get, which is fine, as long as you know about that in the planning stages.

Take some time to check things out in your neighborhood. There might be a tiny specialty food store or an ethnic delicatessen lurking on some side street that you didn't even know about. The grocer who has a reputation for less than adequate produce may have an excellent meat department. Your fish store may offer an amazing array of sauces and condiments. The owner of your corner liquor store may turn out to be a wine mavin.

Ask questions; if you don't know how to choose a perfect eggplant, the green grocer will probably be delighted to tell you. Some large grocery stores even employ home economists, who jump at the chance to describe the unique pungency of arugula, and to tell you how it is used in salads, where it comes from, how it got its name, and when in history it was first used.

HERE'S THE PLAN

Once your assessment is complete, you can move on to the next stage of planning: defining the job. What is the goal? What, exactly, needs to be done? How can it be broken down? What are the obstacles? What are the resources? Who is the available personnel?

The overall goal, of course, is to breathe a little life into your marriage by means of an elegant meal together, without the children, in a cozy little romantic setting in the privacy of your own home, with both of you feeling relaxed and ready to tune in to each other. What exactly needs to be done? Well. Where do we begin?

There are three main categories of tasks. The first, prominent under the "obstacles" heading, is taking care of the children. The second is shopping, preparation, and clean-up for dinner. The third is ambiance.

In your planning committee meeting, over your power breakfast on Saturday morning, come up with a list of specifics in each category. Does a child have a dance lesson that day? Does your menu require an exotic ingredient which can only be found at the Oriental grocery across town? Are you out of candles?

THINGS TO DO

The question of what to do with your children while you are trying to be romantic with each other is addressed in detail in Chapter Five. The questions of how to get them to help out in the kitchen and what to feed them are addressed in Chapters Three and Four. Our purpose here is to point out that all of those things, plus all the other aspects of their day, must be considered in the planning. Someone has to pick up the movie from the video store.

Schedule your children's day, including naps, mealtimes, and activities, around the other things on your list. If someone is needed to take a three year old to the park, then someone else should probably go across town to the Oriental grocery. If someone will be baking French bread with the help of the six year old, then someone else should rent the video and buy the candles. If the twelve year old's Little League team is in the finals of the state championship tournament that day, you both have to go; plan to order out for your special dinner (see Chapter Eight). None of this is difficult, it just requires forethought.

The tasks associated with your dinner depend on the menu. Each menu in Part Two contains a list of ingredients which should be purchased the day of your dinner, and instructions for how to prepare much of the meal in advance during the day, or well in advance to freeze. Later in this chapter you will find suggestions for ingredients with a long shelf life which you can keep on hand to minimize last minute shopping. Select your menu and check your cupboards and freezer before you start dividing up the shopping and cooking.

Don't forget the wine. Check Chapter Seven for wine and cocktail suggestions, and make sure you have what you need. If not, include a trip to the liquor store in your planning, and don't forget the less obvious ingredients such as hazel nuts, maraschino cherries, lime juice, and coarse salt for margueritas.

Now for the ambiance, by no means a minor factor. You want aesthetic pleasures for all of your senses. Select your music. Decide whether you want an eclectic sound track, or only tenor saxophone, for example, and stack up the tapes or compact discs in a convenient place. Set up that small card table in front of the fireplace, and cover it with a lacy cloth (or a colorful quilt, a large paisley scarf, a rag rug, or your grandmother's faded floral kitchen cloth). Set out lots of candles. Build a fire, ready to light. Add fresh flowers to your shopping list, and assign someone to arrange them. Hang your silk kimono out to air, and don't forget to schedule time for a quick shower or soak in the tub.

TIRED YET?

Feeling overwhelmed already? Does all this work raise the specter of starvation and exhaustion? Are you thinking that maybe you really ought to try that baby sitter again, the one who left the lipstick marks in a suspiciously familiar shade on your telephone mouth-piece, and the mysterious stains on your living room couch? Or maybe a dinner of macaroni and cheese and an early bedtime sounds pretty good to you right now.

Don't despair. Working together is an end in itself. Meeting the challenge of creating a special time and place together, in spite of everything, is invigorating. Here is an opportunity to be together in pleasant anticipation of even more fun later on, kind of like being engaged. And, by planning well and doing a little advance work, you can be transformed from frumpy, hungry parents to glamorous lovers eating the finest cuisine within minutes of closing your children's bedroom doors.

PROPS YOU'LL NEED

Drinking champagne out of old jelly jars can be very romantic, depending on your mind set. Sparkling crystal isn't the point; making the evening special is. So if jelly jars have some kind of significance in your relationship, and will add to your enjoyment of champagne, use them with pleasure.

Whatever the choices you make, developing a collection of special things to use on special nights adds to the fun. Think back. Did you meet while playing together on your company softball team? Just the other day we saw a set of highball glasses with balls, bats, and mitts on them in a second-hand store. Was *Casablanca* your favorite movie? Set out a pack of Camel straights; you don't have to smoke them. Do you dream of photographing wild animals in Kenya? Look for dessert plates painted with zebras and gazelles.

Buy only two, though. These things are private. Don't use them for any purpose other than your romantic time together, and don't share them with any one else. In fact, don't even tell any one else; face it, who else but the two of you could fully appreciate your eccentric tastes? Objects have meaning only in the context of your life. Your experiences give them meaning, not the other way around. Not everything you use will be deeply significant, but it should bear some resemblance to your preferences and your life.

Give special dinnerware gifts to each other for birthdays or anniversaries, or choose things together, sneaking a wink or a kiss when the salesperson turns away to ring up the sale. Here are some general ideas.

Candle holders and flower vases are pretty basic. You'll need a selection, so that you can match them to the season, and the degree of formality of your menu and your mood. Baskets in a variety of sizes, shapes, materials, and degrees of antiquity are helpful for everything from canapes to bread to chocolate truffles. A wine carafe is a nice touch. If you enjoy martinis, by all means invest in the proper glassware. Espresso really requires those cute little cups.

Use your wedding china, if you like, or collect place settings for two of more exotic stuff. The same for table linens; again try for enough variety to accommodate all possible moods and seasonal changes. You don't have to stick to tablecloths and place mats, either. Silk scarves and paper doilies work very well.

Go to a restaurant supply store for one of those huge pepper mills. If you are tea drinkers, you will be thrilled with the variety of tea pots out there in the retail world, from the unique to the bizarre. Brandy or cognac is better out of a snifter; but you probably don't need the rack with the little candle to warm it. (Warm it in the palms of your hands, for each other). Once you get started, the sky's the limit, or perhaps your storage space is the limit. In any case, have fun with your props and scenery.

THE PANTRY

Stock your kitchen with special dinners in mind. Some possibilities:

Though fresh seafood is preferable, high quality frozen seafood works fine in most recipes, and your freezer is handier than the seafood store.

The same is true for frozen berries; fresh are definitely better, but a bag of high quality frozen raspberries, thawed with a few drops of a fruity liqueur in a cut glass bowl and spooned over cheesecake is nothing to quibble about.

Some varieties of wild mushrooms are available dried. When rinsed under cold water and soaked in wine, they add an exotic, nymphs-in-the-wood flavor to the tamest of dishes. Try a few morels or porcini sautéed in butter and added to the potatoes in Chapter Sixteen.

Likewise, wild rice, with its long, thin, almost black grains redolent of forests and lakes, is perfect with fish or fowl in front of the fire on a chill autumn night. You could substitute it for the rice pilaf in Chapter Fifteen.

Experiment with vinegars, mustards, and sauces. A nearly infinite variety exists, eliminating any excuse for a boring salad dressing, marinade, or shrimp sauce. Many finer grocery stores and gourmet shops also offer a variety of canned soups, on the opposite end of the spectrum from your basic chicken noodle, and definitely worth trying.

Soup to nuts, as they say; don't forget the nuts. A few slivered almonds or cashews dress up a vegetable dish; pecans or hazelnuts add to a dessert. Store nuts in tightly sealed containers, and buy them in small quantities.

Keep a well stocked shelf of spices and dried herbs. Include different forms of the same spice; whole allspice, for example, used to flavor soups, stews, and gravies, serves a very different purpose from ground allspice, which is used in baking. Try for a full range; black pepper is just as important as saffron. Try some that you've never tried before, or, better still, never heard of. If possible, locate a store which sells herbs and spices in bulk. They are fresher, cheaper, and they keep better.

Garlic, shallots, leeks, parsley, whole parmesan cheese, lemons, and limes keep longer than you might think in your refrigerator, and their flavors are essential.

And then there's chocolate. If you love it, seek it out in all its forms. You need little chocolate liqueur cups, chocolate bars, chocolate truffles, chocolate ice cream, and chocolate sauce. You need powdered chocolate, unsweetened chocolate, semi-sweet, bittersweet, and German sweet. You need chocolate chips and chocolate mints, chocolate roses, chocolate bunnies, and chocolate kisses. Shave slivers of a sweet chocolate bar onto your dessert, whatever it is. Sprinkle a little cocoa powder on the frothed milk in your cappuccino. Share a truffle (or a box of them) at bedtime. You get the idea.

You don't have to be a wine connoisseur, but it's nice to have a couple of bottles of decent wine around. Stock red, white, and champagne. Stock sherry or port, cognac and cordials, as well as whatever you like for cocktails. See Chapter Seven for suggestions.

COSTUMES

Now it's the costumer's turn. In keeping with the mood you are trying to create, wear something that is comfortable, but at the same time a bit on the elegant side, however you define elegant. Your sweat suit or flannel nightgown won't do, although that's not far from the right idea. See if you can upgrade it just a little — a velour sweat suit, maybe, or a flowing hostess gown.

Here is another opportunity to give each other gifts. Again it makes no difference how much or how little you spend, as long as you have fun with the idea. You might find the perfect velvet smoking jacket at a garage sale, or bring back an embroidered silk kimono from your latest trip to San Francisco or New York, or order something you like from one of the numerous catalogues your mail carrier brings.

Take a little time to get into character. Some time between the end of your children's supper and the beginning of your cocktail hour, take turns making the transition. A quick shower or a ten minute soak in bubble bath before you change clothes does wonders for your mood and your sense of anticipation, just as it used to before a big date.

Let the Music Begin

Music is the most effective mood setter there is. Start it before you start your cocktails or hors d'oeuvres, and keep it going throughout the evening. You could invest in a disc changer, which holds up to five compact discs, and plays them continuously. Or, you could take the time to make a romantic dinner tape, or several of them, with your very favorite music, or with a mixture of styles and moods. Whatever music you choose, make sure your evening ends with something you both agree is utterly romantic.

Few things are as personal, as emotional, and as closely guarded as musical tastes. By all means indulge yours fully on special dinner nights, and also take the opportunity to expand your horizons. Public libraries lend out records and compact discs, if you are wary of uncertain purchases. Borrow from friends whose tastes differ from yours, and learn what you can from radio and TV. Build your own collection. It's part of the adventure. We offer here a very short list, meant to jog your imagination, not to limit your options and certainly not to impugn your taste.

Whether you love opera or hate it, try Luciano Pavarotti. His four volumes of *Opera Classics* is delightful as background music, especially if your dinner has an Italian flair. *Momma*, a collection of Italian folk songs, is even better — light, happy, and perfectly wonderful.

Vladimir Horowitz' *The Last Recording*, with piano selections from Chopin, Haydn, Liszt,and Wagner, is powerful, emotional, and very romantic. It's also of highly superior sound quality, according to the audiophiles, which we are not, but we know what we like.

Andreas Vollenweider (*White Winds, Caverna Magica, Dancing with the Lion*) has a mysterious, other-worldly quality, which, as it happens, we first heard in the delivery room when our oldest child was born. Our obstetrician felt that the music would ease the child's transition into this world, which it probably did; he was an amazingly peaceful baby.

Andreas Vollenweider continues to ease our transition into a romantic frame of mind. So does Keith Jarrett's *The Köln Concert*, a flight of unbridled imagination on the piano.

Since so much variety is available on CD, the possibilities are endless. You can renew a taste for the old Kingston Trio or the Beatles, if you care to, or discover what was so funny about Tom Lehrer. You can travel to any country in the world, listen to whales or bird calls or the ocean or the sounds of a tropical rain forest. You can find out what this New Age stuff is all about. Gregorian chants, African drums, and Broadway show tunes each have a unique role to play in creating ambiance. Try something really unusual, or go back to your musical roots, but keep the music playing.

The point, which we shall make again in case it got lost in the flurry of planning and shopping, is to reconnect with each other. The more energy you can put into planning, the greater your sense of anticipation and excitement, and the greater the pay off when you sit down together in the candlelight. Use your imaginations, your experiences, and your preferences to fill in all the blanks.

Chapter 3

YOUR CHILDREN CAN HELP

*Y*ou have children. You need romance. We all know that children and romance coexist poorly. So the idea of children helping to create a setting for romance raises some questions, like, "How?"

The simple answer is that of course they can't really help. The actual romance part is of course strictly between the two of you, although the benefits of it extend to the whole family since you end up with a lot more love at your disposal.

The more complicated answer is that they can help, in their own way, if you make it possible. They can help plan and prepare your special dinner, and one of their own, in ways that suit their ages and abilities, and they benefit from doing it. You don't make them help, you offer them an opportunity to get in on the fun. You let them know they are on the team. On a well managed team, everybody plays.

Even in the throes of their drive towards independence, children need to know they belong. They need to be appreciated. They need to feel valued. They don't like being left out. Give them a job on the family team, encourage them, praise them, spend time with them, give them an allowance. They will help out, and enjoy it.

TEAMWORK

Even on a team where everyone plays, not everyone is the ace pitcher. The toddler's main job, for instance, is to create enough distractions in the household to make all the other jobs sufficiently challenging. But toddlers also have a great time throwing toys in the basket, trash in the trash can, and nuts in the cookie dough, and these are valuable skills. If you encourage their efforts, they will be making the cookies themselves in a few short years, and think it's fun.

Fun, like beauty, is in the eye of the beholder. We once read somewhere that the key to happiness is a capacity to enjoy doing what you have to do. This ability to blur the lines between work and play is a perspective you may not have achieved in your approach to cleaning the toilet or earning a living, but if you think about the pleasures of cooking, it begins to make sense.

Breaking eggs, for example, is fun. Sifting flour is fun. Kneading bread dough is fun. Watching little ribbons of pasta emerge from the pasta machine is fun. Taking a fragrant cake or golden brown loaves of bread or a home-made pizza out of the oven is fun. Of course, the anticipation of eating adds a certain depth and substance to the fun of cooking.

Being a member of the cooking team is fun, too. You get that sense of belonging from working together. You get a feeling of accomplishment from performing a life-giving task. You get to eat. From a child's point of view, it's even better. They get to do grown-up work in the company of the people they love the most, they get to make a big mess (be prepared for this when you start cooking with your children), and they get to try new things. Convincing children to try new foods can be a hard sell, unless they have helped cook.

YOUR ATTITUDE

It is not only your approach to cooking, but to family life, and to life in general, that your children will absorb. If you harbor a secret belief that you really will win the lottery, which really will solve all of your life problems, you can bet that is what your children will pick up on, not all that stuff you tell them about working hard and doing well in school. If "life is hard and then you die" sums up your basic point of view, your children will turn out to be joyless drudges or motorcycle dare-devils. Different from you as your children are, and as little influence over them as you may feel you have, it is nevertheless your view of the world that most affects theirs.

Frightening? You bet. If you ever find yourselves wondering what your children will be telling their psychotherapists in twenty years, that's it.

Managing the family team is looking harder and harder. You have to make sure that everyone plays. You have to make sure that they all play to the best of their abilities. You have to praise them for doing it. And, you are responsible for the development of your players' psyches. Not only that, but your own experience with family life also depends on the tone you set.

YOU'RE ON THE SAME TEAM

The big game is not the Parents vs. the Kids, though we've all had days when it seemed that way. Instead, you can all work together towards common goals.

Take your goal of finding romantic time with each other. Though you can do a great deal to disguise it, the fact remains that your trysts will take place in the context of your family life. Though you can try to pretend otherwise for a few precious hours, your children are unquestionably part of the reality you live with. Though you can aim for sense of escape from it all, your romantic dinners are not separate from your daily life.

On the contrary, they represent a particular approach to daily life, an approach that looks for the adventure and the fun. Enlist your children in the search. Help them, and they'll help you. Join them, and they will be less likely to thwart you when you need time alone.

Set a family goal of having fun. It's more than just a nice thing to strive for, it is at the very core of what holds you together. This is survival. Be straightforward about it. Go about it the same way you go about perfecting your backhand or learning to appreciate modern art or getting that promotion. Set aside time to work on it. Read about it. Learn about the obstacles. Find out how the pros do it. Concentrate. And practice.

PLANNED FUN

Spontaneity is certainly a wonderful thing, but, life with children being what it is, the truth is that not much happens unless you plan it. Plan your family fun seriously, just like you plan your squash games or your conversations with the boss. Schedule regular times, for the family as a whole, for various factions and subgroups within the family, including the two of you, which we've already discussed in detail in Chapters One and Two.

Think up catchy phrases if you can. We've never been able to get past "Fun Thing with Family Night" or "Fun Thing with Daddy Day," but it doesn't matter; the message will be clear. Your children are nice people whose company you enjoy; you find it worthwhile to set aside time just to be with them; their interests interest you; you want to pass on to them what you know; each member of the family deserves special time and attention.

It doesn't have to be a big deal. Throwing a ball around in the back yard, taking a trip around the block on the tricycle, or spending half an hour in the Children's Room at the library are just as important to young children as a day at the zoo or those heavily advertised events at the local auditorium which you need a second mortgage on the house in order to attend. What children need is to be able to count on time with you in a predictable way.

It takes a long time for children to grasp the idea that parents have a life apart from them. Our children were shocked to learn that we didn't go right to bed after tucking them in. Part of the tricky balancing act of parenting is to get across both the idea that the entire family is a unit of which each member is an integral part, and the idea that parents survive parenthood only by spending substantial amounts of time away from their children. Planning fun activities for the whole family, and for various designated subgroups, gets the message across.

KITCHEN COMMAND CENTER

Which brings us back to the idea of your romantic little dinners at home, an excellent case in point.

If you go into your kitchen right now (unless you're already in there reading) you will probably find someone's homework spread out on the table, someone else's flute music propped up on the counter, an assortment of blocks and stuffed animals on the floor, a selection of art work on the refrigerator, and somewhere a stack of bills, notes, reminders, recipes, phone numbers, brochures, school directories, messages, and magazines folded open to articles you didn't want to forget about. The kitchen is where you live. Since everyone is in there all the time anyway, why not put them to work?

Only the kitchen contains that compelling combination of comfort and fascination, of routine and change, of work and play, of single purpose and all-purpose. Whether it's a little person helping out by stacking up canned goods as high as possible on the floor, or a somewhat bigger person standing on a chair to stir the muffin batter, or a still bigger person finishing off the last of the milk directly from the carton while still wearing the in-line skates, the kitchen is where they all want to be.

TEACH THE KIDS TO COOK

This is not an opportunity to be missed. Hand that energetic young skater an eggbeater, and stand back. Start them as young as you can, keeping in mind the limitations in both attention span and coordination of the youngest team members, but still capitalizing on their genuine desire to be helpful and to be in on the action.

Before you begin, face a few realities. They will make a mess. Part of your task is to teach them how to get most of the flour into the bowl, but that's advanced stuff for a three year old. You also have to teach them that cleaning up is part of the fun. But don't make the mistake of assigning a child exclusively to the cleanup detail. Many a promising cook has been lost to the dishwater in the kitchen sink.

Don't rush. Your over-all goal is to teach children not only how to cook, but how to enjoy it. No one learns well under pressure, and no one teaches well in a hurry. The time you spend now, not to mention the practice in stretching your tolerance and your patience, will pay off later.

Encourage and reward any and all attempts to be helpful. Don't require more than your young child is willing to do; if the only fun part is rolling out the pizza crust or sprinkling the cheese on top, don't make them do anything else. However, as they get older and more independent in the kitchen, do require that a job that is started be completed, including cleanup.

Add some fun. Forget what your mother told you; let your kids play with their food. Try cutting slices of watermelon, cantaloupe, and honeydew with cookie cutters, for instance. Look for the unusual shapes: a bat (baseball and the kind that flies), a cat, a whale, a seal, a bird, a giraffe, an elephant, a cloud, a leaf, the new moon, a star, a rocket ship. Arrange the shapes in a pattern on a plate, or mix them in a bowl with some berries.

Make a green salad with a leaf lettuce face, alfalfa sprout hair, cucumber slices for eyes, a mouth made of sweet red pepper slices, and a radish for a nose. A pizza face is fun, too; use mushrooms, green peppers, tomato slices, pepperoni, and green and black olives. Watch how the face changes as it bakes. Turn chocolate cupcakes into little monsters with the help of black licorice strings, red hots, and those little round silver sugar pellets.

Give a hot dog pickle slice legs. Make sandwiches of white, whole wheat, and dark pumpernickel bread; cut off the crusts and cut the sandwiches into squares, rectangles, and triangles. Arrange them to make a house, a barn, or a castle. Children love the novel, the bizarre, and the unexpected. Playing with food is not only fun all on it's own, it is a great way to learn creative cooking.

SAFETY POINTS

Just as you teach your children from the earliest possible ages about safety in the bath tub, on the playground, and while crossing the street, teach them about safety in the kitchen. Kitchen tools and appliances may be fun to use, but they are not toys, were not designed for little hands, and, just like the bath water, can be life threatening without proper precautions.

With the proper precautions and supervision, though, children are safe in the kitchen, and learning to cook can be as much a part of their lives as learning to bathe. You would never leave a toddler alone in the bath, but you can count on your six year old to wash him or herself, wipe out the tub, and hang up the towel; kitchen safety also depends on your judgement. Learn the rules yourself, and teach your children until it becomes second nature.

Make sure all electrical appliances are in perfect working order and that you are thoroughly familiar with instructions for their use. Unplug them as soon as you are finished with them and make sure your hands are dry when you do, as well as when you plug them in.

Knives that are sharp enough to work well are safer than knives too dull to cut properly, but they must be handled carefully. Pick up a knife only by the handle, hand it to another with the handle first. Cut only with the blade down, only on a cutting board. Do not leave sharp knives in the sink.

Always turn pot and pan handles in towards the stove, not outward where an inquiring four year old can reach up and pull them down. Always turn off stove burners and the oven as soon as you are finished with them. Let steam escape from a hot dish or pan by opening the lid away from you. Keep a supply of potholders and oven mitts handy and use them every time you reach for something on the stove, in the oven, or in the microwave.

Respect the microwave. It is so easy to use that its dangers may seem minimal, but they're not. Dishes and food get very hot in a microwave. Wrappers and packaging may be difficult for children to remove. A heavy microwave dish is easy for a child to drop. Food could end up under-cooked unless instructions are followed precisely.

Which leads to our final point. No young child belongs in the kitchen alone, and even older children who know the ropes belong in the kitchen only when an adult knows what they will be doing. Cooking as a family activity is safe and fun for even the youngest members.

BEGINNER'S CLASS: AGES THREE TO SIX

This is Textures 101. Haul a chair over to the counter, tie a large apron over your three year old, and carefully wash those little hands. Flour, sugar, chopped nuts, yeast, dough, lentils, and egg shells all have the same allure as sand at the beach, finger paints, or modelling clay. Who do you think invented Play Dough, if not a parent with a meal to prepare and a preschooler to entertain?

They love to get their hands in things. They love to pour things from one container into another. They love to count. Their curiosity knows no bounds. They make up in enthusiasm what they may lack in expertise. Choose their tasks carefully, keep them short with immediate results, and you will have a good helper.

A three year old is fully capable of breaking eggs, but probably not in a way you would find truly helpful. But even at three your little assistant can pour, sprinkle, or add ingredients which have already been measured. Older preschoolers can measure dry ingredients, and count out cups or tablespoons. They can all help knead or stir, wash salad greens, scrub vegetables, or throw a handful of chopped celery into the meatloaf and squish it together.

Apprenticeship: Ages Six to Nine

Now we're getting somewhere; these kids can read. Not only that, they're bigger, stronger, more confident, and they know a thing or two — like how to handle a hot pan or a sharp knife. They can face a more complex set of instructions, and stay with a task longer. They are beyond the mere tactile experience and into the finished product. They can assemble and mix a variety of ingredients, they can turn the oven to the right temperature, they can learn how to use the microwave and other appliances.

They can break an egg properly, and maybe even separate it. They are strong enough to squeeze a lemon, and to use a rolling pin or knead dough with some effectiveness. They can peel carrots and potatoes. After passing Beginning Cutting, they can slice vegetables. Plopping cookie dough onto a cookie sheet or noodles and sauce into a casserole, sliding it in to the oven, timing it, and pulling it out with a pair of oven mitts are nothing to them now.

Buy your eight year old one of the many children's cookbooks that are available, and ask for help in menu planning and grocery shopping. Give them the responsibility (with guidance as needed) for deciding on some family menus, and for their own menu on your special dinner nights. If they don't want to miss out on the pasta they helped to make, but can't quite deal with garlic yet, help work out a suitable modification of the grown-up menu.

Master Chefs: Ages Nine to Twelve

You can hang up your apron by now. Your new role is Advisor to the Chef, so back off, get out of the kitchen, and get a life. Gaining momentum in their quest for independence, children in this age group find it intrinsically rewarding to plan and prepare not only their own meals, but also their own lives, and everyone else's life, too. If they have had some earlier training and experience in the kitchen, they are well prepared to do so (make some of their own meals, that is; they still need considerable guidance in the life department).

Allow them to take part to whatever extent they like in the preparation of your special dinner, and give them the responsibility for their own dinner that night. Cheesecake, pound cake, or short cake, beautifully shaped baguettes or rolls, baked chicken breasts with a mushroom sauce — not much in the kitchen is beyond them, if they choose to take it on.

ONE FOR ALL

You have created an atmosphere of teamwork and cooperation in your household. You have created an appreciation for the fun part of working hard, and an understanding of the importance of planning fun times. You have taught your children to look for the adventure in life, and in food; you have taught them how to cook. You set aside special time on a regular basis for your children, yourselves, and various combinations.

This is a framework for a very enjoyable family life, in which all participants can get what they need. This is the answer to the question at the beginning of this chapter; your children can help, once you make it possible.

Chapter 4

FEEDING THE CHILDREN

*C*hildren's concept of food is different from ours. Take the time our toddler, thankfully a toddler no more, methodically mashed a banana into the front of his corduroy overalls. He paid special attention to the folds in the fabric, so that certain parts of those overalls were never again free of mashed banana. Then there's his brother, whose primary criterion for an excellent meal is that it can be consumed quickly. He dislikes bagels, large apples, and soup for only one reason: they all take too long to eat.

So planning children's meals is a different sort of exercise from imagining gourmet treats for yourself. It's not a difficult exercise, once you learn to think like a child. Children can certainly appreciate creativity, innovation, and the unexpected; on the other hand, they tend to want their meals to be predictable, they find security in the routine and repetitious, and they will pick an old favorite over the unknown every time.

You can have your children plan their own meals, as we discussed in the previous chapter, but they need guidance. They need a basic nutritional education (you know, the four food groups) as well as a gastronomic spirit of adventure. Start with the idea of variety, and move towards the idea of experimentation. Bring them to the grocery store. Allow them some say in family menu planning; how much say depends on how old they are and, naturally enough, on what they say. You have veto power, along with the responsibility to teach about balanced meals and to impart an appreciation for fine cuisine.

PICKY, PICKY, PICKY

In many households, including ours, the best techniques for inspiring a flair for drama at the table, not to mention sound nutritional practices, fall short. Some children are just fussy eaters. They are adamant about refusing anything with a strange name or weird color or suspicious aroma. While this has its advantages — life is very predictable — it lacks joy.

Passing on your enthusiasm for shrimp, mushrooms, or pesto sauce may not be easy, but it is a necessary challenge if you want your children to approach food as something more than a waste of their time.

You can change those timid souls who enter the kitchen holding their noses and saying "What's for dinner anyway? Something smells yukky!" into gourmets willing to take on blue cheese, eggplant, and sardines with pleasure and panache. But it could be a slow process, and you all need to eat in the meantime. Adopt a subtle approach. As a general rule (except, of course, on special dinner nights), don't make more than one meal; those who object to the sauce can eat their pasta plain.

Don't worry that your fussy eater will be undernourished. If presented with enough variety, children will eventually get what they need, though maybe not in one meal. The concern is more about the quality of their lives, and yours. How sad to be limited to macaroni and cheese and hot dogs for the rest of one's days, or to be served it when you visit the homes of your grown children. It's worth it to invest the effort now.

GIVE THEM CHOICES

Everyone has favorite foods, although the more adventurous eaters have a larger repertoire. A major purpose of your romantic dinners is to eat some of your favorite foods. Another major purpose is to be in a separate part of the house from your children while you do so.

You can include your children in the general festivities by giving them more or less free reign with regard to their favorite foods that night. Though you cannot allow an entire meal of popsicles or popcorn or popovers, you can encourage your children to combine some of their favorite fruits, vegetables, noodles, potatoes, buns, fish, fowl, meats, cheeses and ice cream into a more or less nutritionally complete meal.

MODIFIED ADULT MENU

It may be that they are intrigued by your menu, which is likely if they have helped in any of the preparation. If you are reluctant to share some cherished delicacy (home-grown asparagus has been decreed "too good for kids" in our household, partly as a ploy to get the kids to try some, which backfired, but also because the season is so short and it's so delicious) or if you know for a fact that they will reject some key ingredient, think of some modifications.

Many children object to foods being mixed together, or even touching each other on the plate. A little pile of pasta, a little pile of green beans, a little pile of green and red peppers, and a few shrimp on the plate may be acceptable, while the combination as described in Chapter Eleven may not. Olive oil or lemon juice or salt and pepper may be all the sauce any noodle needs, according to the tastes of a preschooler.

Serve their julienned vegetables raw instead of cooked, if they so desire, leave the garlic off the garlic bread, the brie off the crackers, the pilaf out of the rice, the orange sauce off the chicken and make theirs drumsticks instead of breasts. Serve them the strawberries without the shortcake, or the other way around, or maybe they only want the whipped cream. Use whatever solution is satisfactory and does not require much extra work.

TRY TAKEOUT

Many children are of the opinion that Colonel Sanders, Ronald McDonald, and the pizza delivery person represent a standard of cuisine to which their parents can only aspire. So be it; this is no time to argue about tastes, and there is no reason to ignore any potential resource. Especially if you can manage to restrain yourselves from relying on takeout for everyday fare, eating it will be a special occasion for your children. Remember to plan for any necessary pick-ups when assigning tasks for the day.

If, in exploring your neighborhood for food resources, you discovered some takeout or delivery possibilities that might appeal to your children, a special dinner night is a good opportunity to try them. Here's another chance to work in a bit of that spirit of adventure and discovery that makes life more interesting. And don't overlook frozen pizza or any of the other convenience foods which your grocer makes available; they exist for a reason, and feeding your children separately may well be it.

FANTASY TABLE SETTINGS

Make your children's mealtime into a dress-up game. Obviously, you want to avoid a lot of extra work, but a few props and a little make believe can go a long way.

Spread a blanket on the floor, and tape up a few magazine pictures of bears, foxes, chipmunks, and maybe a sunset, a lake, or mountains. Hand out flashlights, and call it a camp out. If you have camping dishes, use them; otherwise, use pie tins and paper cups. Let the kids wear old flannel shirts and fishing caps, serve trail mix as part of the meal, and pour the milk from a thermos. If you have a fireplace, and have built a fire for your romantic evening, you could offer them s'mores for dessert.

Have a picnic in the back yard. Use paper plates and plastic forks, or picnic dishes. Pack all the food into a basket, use the picnic table if you have one in your back yard, or just spread a plastic table cloth on the grass. Serve lemonade and watermelon, and, if it's one of those long summer evenings and your children are old enough to enjoy it on their own, set up the badminton game.

Invite dolls and stuffed animals to a tea party. Set places for them with a toy china tea set, if you have one. Let the children wear costume jewelry, scarves, or neckties, and serve apple juice "tea" out of cups. Start a conversation about each "guest's" favorite foods, their relationships with each other, or where they lived before coming to live with your children, and see what happens.

What happened in our house was that our children developed an elaborate game of stuffed animal baseball, which they play on the diamond shaped pattern in the rug in their room. They call it Stuffed Animal League. They trade players from team to team. Certain trouble-makers routinely argue with the umpire (a troll) and get physically ejected from the game.

The kids can have their dinner by coming to the "concession stand" for hot dogs, chips, and popcorn, with Cracker Jacks and a chocolate ice cream "frosty malt" for dessert. We try to sneak in some apple slices and carrot sticks, too, even though they know they couldn't get them at the ball park.

If you happen to have some birthday hats and noisemakers left over, have an un-birthday party. Put candles in a piece of cake, or in the mashed potatoes, and sing "Happy Un-birthday to You."

If renting a video is part of your plan for your children's evening, you could let them have dinner while watching it. Call it an overnight trans-Atlantic flight. The video is the in-flight movie, and the TV trays are the seat-back trays. That means you end up being the flight attendant; make sure the travellers get to their hotel rooms before they fall asleep.

If you want to get really far out, try this. Let the kids wear "martian ears" from a novelty store, or antennae made by attaching pipe cleaners with little balls of tin foil on the ends to a girl's plastic headband. Use food coloring to create a meal from outer space: orange milk,say, or blue egg noodles. Just be careful not to trigger the "yuk" response.

We could go on, but enough is enough. Your own children are the best source of whimsical meal ideas. Listen to them carefully, and tap into their imaginations.

TWO STEP-BY-STEP MENUS

Each of the two children's dinners which follow has the advantage of being quick and easy to prepare and being generally appealing to children. The instructions are given in minute detail, so that beginning cooks can learn from them. Use your judgement and consider the amount of time you have available and the skill level of your helpers in deciding how much to cook yourself, and how much to delegate. If you hand the menu over to your ten year old, make sure you are available to answer questions, and to help drain the macaroni in the first menu and the green noodles in the second.

Like the grown-up menus in Part Two, these are meant to serve two (2.5, the average number of children per household, is an awkward number at the table). They can be revised up or down depending on the actual number of children present and their appetites.

MACARONI AND CHEESE
(WITH HAMBURGERS ON BUNS)

We understand that it is possible to create macaroni and cheese from scratch, but, frankly, we don't see what purpose that would serve. The true connoisseurs of macaroni and cheese always prefer the kind that comes out of the box.

Here's the menu: Macaroni and cheese, Hamburgers on buns, Peas, Milk, and Sugared apple slices.

The ingredients are:

One box of macaroni and cheese
Milk and butter or margarine as called for in the instructions
One-half pound of lean ground beef
Two whole wheat hamburger buns
(if you happen to be making the whole wheat rolls in Chapter Twelve, you can use those)
One package of frozen peas
One large crisp apple
Two tablespoons of sugar mixed with one teaspoon of cinnamon
in a small bowl.

Use these utensils: A small sauce pan with a cover, a measuring cup, a small frying pan, a spatula, a covered glass microwave dish or another small sauce pan with a cover for the peas, a paring knife to cut the apple, measuring spoons.

Line up your crew. Have them all wash hands. Here are their instructions: Divide the hamburger in half, and form two patties. Sprinkle a little salt in the small frying pan, place the pan on a burner, and turn the burner to medium. Fill the sauce pan about two-thirds full with water, cover it, place it on a burner, and turn the burner to high.

Carefully place the hamburger patties in the hot frying pan. When the water in the sauce pan boils, add the macaroni from the box, stir, turn the burner to medium-low, and set the timer for the specified amount of time. Meanwhile, measure the milk in the measuring cup, add the butter or margarine, and put it next to the cheese packet in a handy place.

Open the package of peas, and follow the directions on the package for either microwave or stove top cooking. Use a spatula to turn the hamburger patties when they are brown on the bottom (after three or four minutes). When the timer goes off, drain the macaroni, but leave it in the pan. Add the cheese, milk, and butter or margarine and stir well. Leave it on a very low burner, and stir until it is well mixed. Turn off the burner.

Get the ketchup, mustard, and pickles out of the refrigerator. Put an opened hamburger bun on each plate, set the plates near the stove. Set the table with silverware, napkins, and glasses. Pour the milk.

With the spatula, carefully lift the hamburgers out of the pan, and put one on each bun. Turn off all burners. Put some macaroni and cheese and peas on each plate, and bring the plates to the table.

When the crew is finished with supper, have one of them cut the apple into slices, cut the seeds out, and sprinkle the slices with the sugar and cinnamon. If you ever stood around snitching apples slices while someone was making apple pie, you'll recognize this.

GREEN NOODLES AND HAM (WITH APOLOGIES TO DR. SEUSS)

If you happen to be making spinach linguini from the recipe in Chapter Eleven, use that in this meal. Otherwise, your grocer offers all kinds of dried or frozen green noodles; use the family favorite. The variety of colors in this meal makes it especially fun.

Here's the menu: Spinach noodles, ham, candied carrots, chocolate milk, and peppermint bon bon ice cream with chocolate sauce.

The ingredients are:

About one-half of a sixteen-ounce package of spinach egg noodles,
or the equivalent amount of another kind of pasta
Olive oil
Salt and pepper
One pre-packaged and preferably pre-cooked ham slice
(about one-half-inch thick and weighing about one pound)
One tablespoon vegetable oil
Two large carrots
One tablespoon butter
One tablespoon brown sugar
Chocolate milk or powdered cocoa mix
Peppermint bon bon ice cream
Chocolate sauce

Use these utensils: a large sauce pan with a cover, a frying pan large enough to hold the ham slice, a colander, a paring knife, a cutting board, measuring spoons, a carrot peeler, a small sauce pan with a cover or a small covered glass microwave dish for the carrots.

Line up your crew. Have them all wash hands. Here are their instructions: fill the large sauce pan about two-thirds full with water. Put it on a burner, cover it, and turn the burner to high. Peel the carrots, cut them into slices on the cutting board, and put them in the small covered sauce pan with enough water to cover them completely, or in the covered glass microwave dish with just a little water. Put the frying pan on a burner, measure the vegetable oil into it, and tilt the pan so the oil coats the bottom.

Unwrap the ham slice, put it on the cutting board, cut off and discard as much of the fat around the edges as you can. Cut several small slits in the outside edge of the ham slice so it won't curl up in the pan.

If the carrots will be cooked on the stove top, put the cover on the pan, put the pan on a burner, and turn the burner to medium. Cook the carrots for fifteen to twenty minutes, until they are tender. If they will be cooked in the microwave, cover the glass dish, put it in the middle of the microwave, and cook on high for five minutes.

When the water boils in the large sauce pan, add the noodles, and set the timer for the amount of time specified on the package. Put the ham slice in the frying pan, and turn the burner to medium. Cook the ham for about three minutes, or until it begins to turn brown on the bottom. Use a fork to turn it over, and cook on the other side for another three minutes. If the ham is not precooked, cook it for about six or seven minutes on each side.

Set the table with silverware, napkins and glasses, and put the plates in a handy place near the stove. Pour the chocolate milk, or pour the white milk and stir in the cocoa mix.

When the carrots are cooked, turn off the burner or take them out of the microwave, drain the water out, and add the butter and brown sugar to the pan or dish; stir until the butter and brown sugar melt, and the carrots are coated. When the timer goes off, turn off the burner under the noodles, drain the noodles in the colander, put them in a serving bowl, and sprinkle them with a little olive oil and salt and pepper.

Turn off the burner under the ham, use a fork to take the ham out of the pan, and cut it in two on the cutting board. Put one portion on each plate, along with a serving of carrots and noodles.

After the cooks have enjoyed their meal, let them dish up the ice cream, drizzle it with chocolate sauce, and enjoy that!

Chapter 5

OH BOY, BEDTIME!

*I*t's eight o'clock. The lights are low. Vladimir Horowitz plays a Chopin nocturne softly in the background. Wine glasses gleam on a table for two set by the fire. Deep red carnations nod from a cobalt blue bowl.

In the kitchen, mussels sit on a plate, waiting to be steamed into delectability. A Manhattan cocktail waits in its shaker next to the chilled glasses. Delicate smells of garlic and shallots, fresh bread and just-ground coffee foretell culinary pleasures.

The children, adorable in their little plaid pajamas, giggle over their bedtime story. When the story ends, they hug and kiss you, snuggling against your silk kimono or velvety shirt front. Then they climb into their beds, saying "night-night," and "I love you," as you tuck the covers in around them. They yawn sweetly.

You switch off the light, close the door gently, join hands and tiptoe away to your romantic rendezvous. Your home is transformed. Bon appétit!!

Some of you may be skeptical. "Yeah, right," you may be saying. You may have the feeling many of us get from looking through *Architectural Digest* or the Horchow catalogue: this is very lovely, but it doesn't apply to me. Maybe it doesn't, yet. But soon you will be equipped with enough strategies, techniques and tricks to make this scenario, or something very much like it, possible in your home.

WHO'S IN CHARGE?

The main strategy is no trick, just sound parenting. Like the main strategy in getting the kids to help out (see Chapter 3), it has to do with your general approach to family life. Face it, it's your show. You are in charge. You are in the role of a benevolent dictator. Your goal, of course, is to rule for the maximum good of all. In a family, the maximum good of all is best served through laws of the land that are based firmly on structure and routine.

By providing your family with structure and routine, you provide a sense of security and predictability for your children, and a great deal of freedom for yourselves to do what you need to do, and what you want to do. By making small changes in the routine, you create a special occasion. This is the basic idea behind the romantic dinner plan.

THE FAMILY SCHEDULE

Start early. All of the baby books that we read — and we read a lot of them — couldn't say enough about getting the baby into some kind of routine. The advice runs the gamut from establishing tightly controlled four-hour feedings to trying to figure out your baby's routine, and following that. Whatever your style, you must somehow create some order from the formless mass your life with a new baby has become.

It helps if you are a person who finds comfort in schedules. If "this is meatloaf, so it must be Tuesday" is among your organizing principles, you are already a few steps ahead. For most of us, however, even if we are capable of keeping a schedule for ourselves, fitting a baby, or a family, into one is a daunting prospect.

The kind of structure you and your family need depends on two things: the kind of structure in which you find comfort, and the kind of structure imposed by external things, like your job.

Let's say your preferred routine is to stay up reading until the wee hours one night, and to have your supper in bed, falling asleep immediately afterward, the next. And, let's say, you have to be at work between nine and five every Monday through Friday. You see the potential for problems. Similarly, you may be a meatloaf-on-Tuesdays type married to someone who never heard of Tuesday. Or, you might be a take-it-as-it-comes parent with a baby who really wants to be fed every four hours. In all these cases, compromise and balance are your friends.

ACCLIMATE BABY

A baby's routine is built around the most basic of comfort factors, eating and sleeping. It is built around one external factor: you, and the rest of the family. Your first task in providing a workable structure is to discourage the baby from being awake during the time you like to be asleep. Most of us manage to accomplish this fairly quickly. We do it through a combination of figuring out what suits the baby, and ruthlessly imposing our own will.

Having mastered Sleeping Through the Night, you graduate to Regular Meal Times. Regular meals are good for your health (all the diet books say so), and essential to a predictable family life. Your meals need not be regular according to any schedule but your own, but life is a lot easier if mealtimes are signposts and not meandering streams. Most babies will catch on to the idea of eating at certain times with some encouragement, and are a lot happier for it.

Gradually, your baby will have more and more time available that isn't taken up with eating and sleeping. This gives you a chance to build playtime and other activities into the daily routine. You will find that regular playtime, regular mealtime, and regular sleep time all work together, each making the others work better.

We don't recommend trying a romantic dinner at home if you have a new-born. A new-born's needs outweigh any needs you may have for the time being, and besides, they're awfully unpredictable. But, as soon as you think that your baby will sleep for several hours at a time between, say, eight and midnight, go for it. Plan your date night around the baby's sleeping and eating schedule. Since most babies fall asleep right after they eat, feed the baby just before you want to start your hors d'oeuvre.

ADJUST TODDLER'S SCHEDULE

As the months pass, and as your baby's waking hours increase, you can begin to make small changes in the routine which will make your planning easier on Special Dinner days. Stretch the afternoon play time a little, and you may get an earlier bedtime. Add a feeding time late in the day, and your baby may sleep longer.

By the time your baby turns into a toddler, your household routine will be well established. Add a bedtime routine: jammies, snack, brush teeth, story, choose a stuffed animal to sleep with, good-night hugs and kisses, tuck in, and lights out, for instance. Repeating this routine night after night gives your toddler a sense of security, and makes bedtime predictable from the child's point of view as well as from yours.

On romantic dinner days, plan a special toddler activity during the day, and connect it to your plans for the evening: "This is Mommy and Daddy's special night, so it's your special day," you could say. The activity could be as simple as a picnic lunch or an hour at the park, or more elaborate, like swimming at the YMCA, or, for older toddlers, a movie. It doesn't matter what it is, just so it's fun and slightly out of the ordinary.

Add a short walk or bike ride, some singing and dancing games, or some other silly game that you make up together (a tickle party, for example) before you start the bedtime routine. Be careful, though; the goal is a sleepy toddler, not an over stimulated one. Set a clear time limit before you begin, and, as with all other limits you set, stick with it.

Talk to your toddler. Talk about how important he or she is, and about how important family time is. Talk about how important it is to you to spend time together as a couple, too. Talk about these things often. It may go right past your toddler, but you'll feel like you're doing something helpful.

BRIBE TAKING: AGES THREE TO SIX

By age three, variations in the usual routine become very helpful on romantic dinner days. A three year old can skip an afternoon nap, if you dare, and stand a pretty good chance of going to bed early. A three year old can enjoy doing simple tasks in the kitchen. A three year old is capable of true cooperation, and even of delayed gratification. A three year old can be bribed.

Your strategy with preschoolers goes beyond the simple techniques designed to make sure they are tired at bedtime. But an active day is still among your most reliable tools, especially if the activities are special in some way. You can include your preschooler as a member of the cooking team, as described in Chapter 3, because they love to help. The idea of creating something nice for Mommy and Daddy intrigues them — at least within the confines of their preschool attention spans.

Having their own favorite meal, helps, too. Not only is it a treat, but it sets the day apart from other days, and adds to the sense of festivity you are trying to create.

Your goal is to change the routine enough to make things interesting, but not enough to be disruptive. You need to add to the appeal of bedtime without adding to your preschooler's already formidable energy level. There are a number of ways to accomplish this. One is outright bribery: "Go to bed now, and stay in bed, and you can watch three cartoons instead of two in the morning."

Or, you could say, "It's eggs benedict and pineapple-orange-mango juice for breakfast for everyone who cooperates at bedtime," though with any luck your child's favorite breakfast will be frozen waffles.

Bribery is certainly not your only trump card. Preschoolers have a joie de vivre, a spirit of adventure, and a sense of wonder unequalled in any other age group. These can be fully exploited by creative parents, to the benefit of all. Here are just a few ideas; if you think about your own child's quirks and idiosyncracies, you will come up with many more.

If you have more than one child, let them trade beds, or trade rooms for the night. They can either bring their favorite blankets and stuffed animals from their own beds, or increase the sense of adventure by using each other's. If they are close enough in age, they might even trade pajamas. Talk it up during the day, so they can look forward to it. Make it a game: "We won't even know who's who in the morning! Boy, will you ever be able to fool us!"

Keep an extra set of sheets, or a comforter, afghan, or bedspread, with a favorite character or motif for use on special occasions. Waldo comes to mind, or the endless list of Disney characters, or baseball, ballet, a coral reef or outer space; retailers supply us with infinite variety. It could be a family artifact — your old blanket from your preschool days, for instance, or a doll or stuffed animal you had as a child. Let your child choose, whether you buy something from a store or catalogue or dig it out of your attic, and keep it special by limiting its use.

Announce a Backwards Bedtime night, and go through the entire bedtime routine backwards. Turn out the lights first. Read the bedtime story by flashlight. Brush teeth twice, once before snack and again afterward. Tuck in the chosen stuffed animal before getting pajamas on. Wear the pajamas backwards. Laugh over those items in the routine that can't be reversed, like how can you get tucked in before you have your jammies on?

These things are fun, and they work, or at least they can work. The bottom line, though, is very simple. As our five year old puts it, the thing that makes him want to go to bed the most is being tired. And that brings us back to the basic principle of structure and routine. A child who has a regular bedtime is likely to be tired when it comes around.

INDEPENDENT: AGES SIX TO NINE

This principle only increases in importance as your children get older. Grade school teachers are adamant about it. If there exists a Manual of Advice Most Often Offered to Parents by Teachers, it consists of two things: read to your child every day, and establish a regular bedtime and stick to it. Though the principle of structure and routine is immutable, the routine itself changes as your children grow.

Children in the early grades have seen something of the big world, and they are beginning to take themselves pretty seriously. They have lots of new skills, from reading to tying their own shoelaces, to applying their own toothpaste, and they solemnly take on new responsibilities to match. They have gotten good at filling their own time, and need considerably less from you in the having fun department. The exploitable characteristics in this age group are self-confidence, independence, and the budding sense of responsibility.

The responsibility of entertaining themselves is one six year olds (and up) take very seriously. They know what they like, and their repertoire of entertainment options expands practically daily as their skills and abilities increase. They can read. They can write stories and illustrate them. They can stage plays. They can draw and paint. They can make up games to play together. They can play Nintendo.

This gives you more possible ways to sweeten their bedtime. On your romantic dinner days, let the children know that they can plan to have some fun after lights out. The illusion of getting away with something gives a first grader great pleasure, so if you can give the impression that their fun will be their secret, so much the better. Just make it clear that they have to leave you alone, and go to sleep on their own. Go through the bedtime routine as usual, complete with hugs and kisses and a ritual tucking in. Provide some supplies:

Buy glow-in-the-dark books. Three good titles are *The Glow in the Dark Night Sky Book* and *The Glow in the Dark Book of Animal Skeletons,* both published by Random House, and *A Very Scary Haunted House,* published by Scholastic, Inc. Supply a flashlight, and be prepared to hear "Ooh, cool" for awhile. Other glow-in-the-dark things, like dinosaur skeletons and white rats, mobiles, and stars you can stick to the ceiling add to the fun.

Let your child build a tent or a fort out of extra sheets and blankets in his or her room, and sleep in it in a sleeping bag. Supply a flashlight. Just make sure the fort is sturdy enough to last until morning, or this plan will backfire.

Encourage late night reading. We were always told that reading under the covers with a flashlight was bad for our eyes, and maybe that is why we need glasses. But it sure was fun, especially the feeling that we were getting away with something. If you believe what your mother told you about it, then allow a reading light to be on for a specified time, making the child responsible for turning it off and going to sleep.

Bring in a tape player, with one or two music or story tapes. Priscilla Herdman's album *Stardreamer* has some wonderful songs and lullabies. Or try Tom Paxton's *The Marvelous Toy,* Jean-Pierre Rampal's *Children's Songs,* Harry Belafonte singing *Day-O,* any recording of Prokofiev's *Peter and the Wolf,* anything at all by Raffi or Wee Sing, and that's just the beginning of a very long list of recordings for children. Children's bookstores have whole walls of book and tape packages, everything from Dr. Seuss to Mother Goose.

We wouldn't want to leave out the possibility of allowing a video after the usual lights out, carefully chosen and short. Do this only if you can do it in a room far away from your tryst, and only if you can count on your children to sneak off to bed after the movie.

ALMOST GROWN-UPS: AGES NINE TO TWELVE

If six year olds are beginning to have a little bit of a sense of responsibility, nine year olds are practically grown-ups. They are more and more in charge of their own lives — and anyone else's life they can get to. Assuming you have provided the necessary direction, you now have a capable first sergeant.

With nine to twelve year olds, it's less important that they be in bed or even in their rooms when you have your romantic dinner, as long as they are somewhere other than where you are and will stay there. They can be fully responsible for their own bedtime routine, and for keeping themselves occupied beforehand, and will probably regard any guidance you offer as interference. You still need to offer some guidance, though, because you want them to go to bed before you do.

Set up a chess or checkers match. Make it best two out of three, or a tournament if you have enough kids, and offer a small cash prize to the winner, payable only if they don't try to involve you in rules disputes. You could do the same thing with Monopoly, Scrabble, Hearts, Cribbage, or any other favorite game. Allow access to the kitchen for popcorn. Specify a time for the match to end.

Get one of those 1,000 piece jig-saw puzzles. Encourage your child to work on it until he or she is bleary-eyed and stumbles gratefully into bed.

Consider inviting a friend for a sleep over. The success of this plan depends on the invited child. For this purpose, you want the kind who turns the other way when you say hello, not the kind who prefers your conversation to your children's company.

If the weather and your neighborhood permit, set up a tent in the back yard. Supply it with sleeping bags, pillows, flashlights, books, a radio or tape player, a deck of cards, and snacks.

You could always rent a video.

SEE, IT WORKED

So, there you are, you two love birds, snuggling on the couch in your elegant lounge wear, sipping cognac, savoring your last bite of chocolate cheesecake, listening to Segovia's final chords fading away. You feel relaxed, refreshed, renewed, and, for the moment, child free. All that planning paid off, and bought you some precious time together. Carry the candles into your bedroom. The night is young.

Chapter ❦
6

HERE WE ARE, WHAT DO
WE TALK ABOUT?

*F*inally! Alone at last. You anticipate some stolen time with your lover, a delicious meal, and after that, who knows? You sip your cocktail and savor your hors d'oeuvre. You are surrounded by music and bathed in candle light. Yet you are struck primarily by the silence at the table.

You begin to cast about in your mind for topics of conversation. The fact that the house needs a new roof hardly seems appropriate. Neither does orthodontia, plantar warts, toilet training, sibling rivalry, lost library books, or any other current concern.

You could bring up the conversation you had just last night with your dear one's mother, who never misses an opportunity to let you know how to do things right, but that could get touchy. The weather? Too impersonal. "Read any good books lately?" No, you know what books your sweetheart has read, you recommended them; you also know the answer to "seen any good movies lately?"

You start to feel a little desperate. This is the person to whom you are closest in all the world, and you can't think of anything to talk about now that you're finally alone. What did you talk about in the old days? What do other couples talk about when they are alone with each other? Is this normal?

LEARNING TO TALK

Next to finding time together, remembering how to talk to each other is the greatest challenge most parents face in their relationship. "We can't communicate," is the most common complaint of couples who go into couples counseling, followed closely by "He doesn't listen to me," and "She doesn't understand me."

For people who are preoccupied with mundane things like earning a living, running a household, and raising children, skills in intimate conversation often degenerate to "It's your turn to do the kids' bath tonight," or "I see we're out of paper towels again." Some parents pretty much stop talking to each other altogether, believing they've heard it all anyway, and having other things to think about.

Many who do talk, fight: "Can't you get it through your thick skull that I've always hated your idiotic mother? Next time she calls, you talk to her!"

"Oh, yeah? Well your mother is no prize either, and neither are you!"

Or they talk about really boring things: "Nice day."

"Sure is. Nicer than yesterday."

Though each of these conversational options has a place in daily life, none offers much potential for relationship growth. Despite the years of sharing the same table and the same bed, the complexities of your partner's personality get more mysterious over time, not less so, especially after the transforming experience of parenthood. As it gets harder to find the time to explore them, it also becomes more important to try. Otherwise, once the kids move out, you'll find yourself married to someone you don't know.

You both need to express thoughts and feelings, and you need to listen to each other. This is hard to do unless you are pretty sure that your partner generally cares about what you think and how you feel. You were pretty sure of that once, or you never would have married each other.

If your intimacy skills have foundered on the rocks of parenthood, you can use your romantic dinners at home as a time to rebuild them. Every relationship has its share of disagreement, displeasure, aggravation, irritation, annoyance, petulance, and boredom, all of which need to be aired. Find another time to do that, though. The goal here is to get intimate without getting nasty, and to keep the conversation interesting without creating conflict. Like on a date.

THE "I-STATEMENT"

If you go to couples counseling to learn how to talk to each other again, the first thing they'll teach you is the "I-statement." You have to stop saying,

"You make me so mad! Why can't you learn to ride the unicycle backwards, like a normal person? And that nose! I thought you went to clown school!"

Instead, you say, "I feel frustrated and embarrassed when I see you ride your unicycle facing forward. I would prefer if you would ride it backwards, like they taught us in clown school." And you leave out the part about the nose, for now, because it's not fair to offer a second criticism before your loved one has had a chance to respond to the first.

It may seem like quibbling over semantics — you're still mad, whether you say "you made me mad," or "I'm mad." But there is a crucial difference. In the first instance, you are blaming your true love for something over which he or she has no control. Tempting as it may be to think so, no one else can cause the feelings you experience, which is something else they teach on the first day of couples counseling.

In the second instance, you are taking the responsibility for your own feelings. Your lover may not be thrilled to learn that not every action on his or her part delights you, but you have a responsibility to express feelings that affect the relationship, and your partner has a right to know about them. Using an "I-statement" is a clear, respectful and positive way to do this.

Its use is not limited to expressing anger:

"I'm frightened when you're out later than you say you will be."

"I'm sad that you're upset with me. I'm sorry."

"I'm happy we planned this time to be together."

"I love you."

Open Ended Questions

On the second day of couple's counseling, you learn about open ended questions. You learn not to try to start a conversation by saying, "So, did your wig fall off in the middle of the backwards unicycle ride, like it did last week?" Your true love could simply reply "Yes" or "No;" end of conversation. Neither do you want to start by saying, "I don't suppose anyone laughed again today," to which your partner could respond with no more than a baleful look, again ending the conversation. Instead, you say, "How did the show go today?" and settle back to hear all the ins and outs of it.

Asking an open ended question implies that you are interested in hearing the answer. To confirm this, you need another skill, called "active listening." In active listening, you don't look down at your soup during the story of how the wig fell off in the middle of the ring, and somehow ended up on top of the pile of Romanian tumblers in the final act. You don't acknowledge the end of the story by saying, "So, read any good books lately?"

Active listening involves eye contact, for starters. It also involves body language, like leaning towards your sweetheart during the most interesting parts. It includes rejoinders which indicate interest. Laugh nicely at the appropriate times, groan at the painful parts. Make little comments and ask leading questions: "You're kidding! Oh, no! What did you do then? Good grief, how did you feel?" Say, "I really admire you for sticking with this" at the end.

SPECIALTY TOOLS

I-statements, open ended questions, and active listening are like your pots and pans, mixing bowls and wooden spoons. You can't run your kitchen without them. But to create some of the more exotic dishes, you need specialty tools — a food processor, say, or the very finest knives in every available size, or a pasta machine. Likewise, if you want to get past mere maintenance in your relationship, you need some fancier communication tools. You need to take a few conversational risks. You need to ask the interesting questions, and give the deeper answers.

When you were dating, you thought of each other as people you wanted to get to know better, and not just in the bedroom, either. You shared your most secret feelings, you revealed your most painful memories and your most cherished dreams, as well as your most mundane daily experiences. You were fascinated by each other's conversation. You did everything you could to get your lover to tell you more. You were charming, witty, empathic, understanding, open, honest, and caring. You laughed at each other's jokes, and dried each other's tears. Do the same now. This is the big date.

SWEET MEMORIES

You have a history together. Shared memories give you an irreplaceable basis for intimacy, but only if you talk about them. Talk about your history together in a way that will teach you more about each other now. You want more than just the facts, although if you have different perceptions of what the facts were, a comparison is always interesting. You want the thoughts and feelings.

"Remember that time," you could start, "when we were climbing the north face of Mt. McKinley? And that ledge gave way under your left foot? What were you thinking right then, knowing that the only thing between you and a rocky death was me holding a rope?"

Or, "Remember that time we decided we should walk to the grocery store, even though it was thundering off to the west and there were reports of tornado touch-downs all over? And we ended up getting way too much stuff, and had to walk home in the pouring rain with hail as big as golf balls carrying five bags of groceries and the twelve-pack? I've always wondered how you felt about me right then, since I'm the one who insisted on walking."

Your memories could be more general. Remember the first place you lived, friends you had, a concert or a play you both enjoyed, or both hated, or one of you hated it and the other loved it. Recall your first date, your wedding day, your wedding night, your first trip together, and your first fight, if no rancor lingers. Remember good times and bad, funny times and sad ones, and times you disagreed. The questions are simple: What were you thinking? How were you feeling? The answers will be more complicated, and filtered through the intervening years.

SHARED DREAMS

Do you dream of money and glory, power and fame, a manageable mortgage, a car that runs? Do you hold on to some hope for a career as a major league pitcher, a *Vogue* model, a British rock star? Do you drive past the big houses on the lake, and imagine yourself living there? Or maybe you see yourself on a farm house porch instead, blissfully shelling peas as the laundry flaps in the breeze and your lover strums a guitar at your feet.

Maybe you work as an accountant, but you know you could be a great painter if only you had the time. Maybe you drive a city bus, but you know that being a tour guide in the Himalayas would suit you better. Maybe you grew up in Kansas, but you know that the Land of Oz is your true home.

Let your imagination run wild, or keep both feet firmly on the ground, but tell each other your dreams. Ask the questions: If you could be anything, live anywhere, travel to any destination, have any life you wanted, what would it be? Why? Who are you, really, behind that work-a-day facade? The answers are revealing; they are not about life as it is, but about life as you think it should be.

Indulge in a little fantasy. Is there a way that dream, or something resembling that dream, could be realized? If you can't earn a living as a great painter, could you take a few art classes through community education? If you can't be a tour guide in the Himalayas, how about a week in the Adirondacks? What if one of you wants the big house in the city, and the other yearns for the farm house porch? Explore the differences, enjoy the contrast, imagine a compromise.

PLANNING THE FUTURE

Twenty years from now, your children, by then well educated, responsible citizens, have grown up and moved out. They have satisfying careers, wonderful spouses, adorable children. They are financially well off, or at least stable. In any case, they are no longer your problem, and once again it is just the two of you.

"You'll be bald by then, just like all your uncles," you could say, "but I'll still love you." Or, "All the women in your family get that flabby skin under the jaw line, and I suppose you will, too, but I won't mind. I'll still love you."

Talk about what you'll do: "It'll be great; we can spend every day at the race track and every evening going over the Racing Form. We'll work out whole new handicapping strategies. We'll go to every track in the country, Saratoga, Aksarben, Santa Anita. We'll see the Kentucky Derby, we'll see all the Triple Crown races, and then we can start on Europe; some of the greatest tracks in the world are in Europe!"

Or, "We'll move to Hawaii, hang out on the beach all day, drink mai-tais, eat poi, never wear shoes except on the golf course."

What will you be like as old people? Will you feel free and adventurous, wise, learned and worldly? Will you travel? Will you take up race-walking, hang gliding, scuba diving? Will you write that novel you've been thinking about since you were a kid?

How will you be with each other? Will you walk contentedly hand in hand through your garden in the evenings, or will you challenge each other to vicious matches on the shuffleboard court? Will you ride up the coast highway on the Harley at sunrise, canoe the white water of the Colorado River, or read poetry to each other in your rocking chairs? Will you still toast each other with glasses of champagne? Will you bring each other sweaters when you're cold, and rub each other's shoulders when you're tired?

What will be important in your lives? With your children gone, your life's work done, where will you find meaning? How will you do things that matter? Will the goal of shooting your age on the golf course be enough of an intellectual challenge, enough of a contribution to society, or will you feel compelled to collaborate on a project to translate the works of Roger Angell into Japanese?

Talk about growing old together. Project your relationship twenty, thirty, forty years into the future. Imagine how the world will change — finally, affordable and safe public transportation; finally a treatment for hay fever that works — and how that might affect you. Or, plan a party for your fiftieth wedding anniversary.

LIVE IN THE PRESENT

Memory, fantasy, and conjecture have their place in your romantic conversation, but don't forget that you live in the present. Talk about that, too. Continue to aim at a level below the superficial, and these conversations will provide the mainstay of your deepening intimacy and a relationship that continues to grow.

Your questions could be very general: "So, how do you feel about the way things are going for us lately?"

Or very specific: "How did you like it last night when I snuck up behind you while you were reading Stephen King and tickled your ear with a feather? I know you screamed and hit me with a sofa pillow, but how did you really like it?"

You could talk about general topics: "I'm in favor of the mayor's decision to lock all the city council members into the jail as a way of drawing attention to the poor conditions there. What's your opinion?"

And about the more intimate side: "You look so sexy when you talk about the city council. I love the way your lip curls, your cheeks flush, and the steam comes out of your ears."

Local politics, world affairs, religion, philosophy, history, art, literature, and sports can all be fun to talk about. It is not necessary that you agree about any of them, only that you find them interesting and can discuss them with pleasure. Your relationship and your daily life are even more fun to discuss, because you can't talk about them on quite the same level with anyone else. The same is true of sex.

You might think that a conversation with each other about sex belongs under the "Dreams" heading, or maybe under "Memories." Maybe you think sex is something you'll get back to once the kids move out. If so, bring it into the present.

"Last time we made love, I really liked it when you...."

"Tonight I'm looking forward to..."

"Touch me there again, just like that."

THE RULES

Though increasing intimacy is part of the goal, don't sacrifice manners for depth. This is not a therapy session, it's a romantic interlude. You want to be appealingly vulnerable, not brutally honest. You want to be fascinating and intriguing, not picky and ridiculous. You want to be charming and witty, not sarcastic and derisive. You want to share a gentle laugh together about your foibles and imperfections, not belittle each other for your annoying failings. You want a deeper understanding of your lover's thoughts, feelings, opinions, and experiences, not a requirement that they agree with yours.

Through your conversation, create an atmosphere of support and acceptance. You can (and should) hash out the inevitable unpleasantness in your relationship at another time, but for tonight, gallantry prevails. Remember that it isn't only the negative feelings about each other, or about your life together, that bear discussion. Tonight is a time to be in love.

Chapter ♦
7

IN THE SPIRIT OF THE EVENING: COCKTAILS AND WINE

"*D*on't drink the bar whiskey, always order your brand."

This bit of wisdom has been handed down for several generations in our family. Its originator certainly drank his share of his brand, and at least enough of the bar whiskey to know the difference.

He ran the municipal liquor store in his small farm town, and prided himself on stocking the widest variety of wines and spirits this side of the big city. He could distinguish the quality of anything in a bottle by sniffing the cork, and did so with great pleasure, though he never again touched a drop after the day in 1949 when a drunk driver broad-sided his car on an icy bridge.

We tell this story by way of saying that there is more than one way to enjoy a drink. A whiff of the bouquet, the clink of ice in the glasses, the gurgle of the liquor as it pours from the bottle, the dark gleam of the bottle itself, its smooth coolness to the touch, and the taste of its contents on the tongue, all go beyond the mere anticipation of an altered state of mind.

ENJOY MODERATION

Since you might feel tipsy just from reading this chapter, we thought it wise to begin with a few caveats. The goal of your romantic evening is to enhance your pleasure in each other, and in your food, and you don't want the experience marred by any of the unpleasant aspects of drinking. Use your own common sense, and some guidelines:

As a general rule, your body can metabolize about one drink an hour; that's one beer, one glass of wine, or one ounce of liquor. Theoretically, if you drank at that pace, you could drink all night, and never get drunk. It's a good rule of thumb, but it's not perfect. There is some build-up effect. Liquors vary in the amount of alcohol they contain. And, most cocktails contain more than an ounce of liquor.

Always measure your cocktails; they taste better, and you know what you're getting. Use lots of ice in the glass; while you don't want a watered down drink, you do want a cold one. The ice improves the taste and somewhat dilutes the effects of the liquor.

Don't fill a wine glass more than about half full. A wine glass is designed so that when you lift it to your lips to drink, you also get to sniff the aroma (the "bouquet"), and double your pleasure. The bigger the wine glass, the bigger the bouquet, not the more wine. Liqueurs and cordials are meant to be consumed in very small quantities, hence those little tiny glasses. They are generally very sweet, and pack a big wallop if you over do it.

Plan on just one cocktail, especially if it has more than one kind of liquor in it, or if you also want wine with dinner. If you plan to start your dinner with a light wine, as we describe in the wine section, and then move on to other wines as the meal progresses, you probably don't want a cocktail, too. On the other hand, a cocktail may be all you want, and perhaps a little brandy with your coffee and dessert.

If you feel by the time dessert comes around that it would not be enhanced by a wine or cordial, just have coffee. If your dessert wine is the one you were looking forward to, plan your earlier drinking accordingly.

If you are (understandably) concerned about drunkenness and waste when you open three different bottles of wine for one meal, remember that you only need a little of each one to enhance the flavor of your hors d'oeuvre, entrée, or dessert. Some vineyards make half bottles available. Look for a device called a "wine saver," which creates a vacuum inside the bottle, so that the wine keeps fairly well for quite a while.

Think of your cocktails and wine as contributing to the ambiance of the evening. Enjoy them the way you enjoy your food, the atmosphere, and each other: savor them slowly.

COCKTAILS

First, a short course in barware. A highball glass, the tall one, is used for drinks made with a mix, such as tonic or club soda. An old-fashioned glass is the short one, and is used for cocktails that are served "on the rocks," (with ice), but are not made with a mix. A double old-fashioned glass is the same thing, but a little bigger. A cocktail glass is cone shaped, and stemmed. It is used to serve cocktails "straight up," that is, without ice. The only other necessary equipment is a cocktail shaker, which is a simple, functional container with no bells and whistles, a shot glass that measures ounces, and a long handled spoon.

Like food and clothing, cocktails have a season. Your palate appreciates deeper, richer flavors (bourbon, for instance), in cold weather, and lighter flavors (gin or maybe rum) in warm weather. Some cocktails, like the Martini, are seasonless. We offer recipes for a few classics.

BOURBON DRINKS

Use a bourbon, such as Jim Beam or Old Fitzgerald, not a blended whiskey, which contains unnecessary, and possibly allergenic, neutral spirits.

For a Manhattan cocktail: fill a cocktail shaker with ice cubes. Measure 3 ounces of bourbon, and 1-1/2 ounces of sweet vermouth; add to the shaker. Add about 1/2 teaspoon of the juice from a bottle of maraschino cherries, and 2 or 3 drops of Angostura bitters. Slowly stir the cocktail, and let it sit for a couple of minutes to achieve the proper "melt." Use a long handled spoon to transfer the ice cubes from the shaker into two double old-fashioned glasses. Add some ice to the glasses if necessary. Pour the cocktails over the ice, and add a maraschino cherry to each glass.

For a lighter bourbon drink, fill a highball glass about half full with ice, measure 1-1/2 ounces of bourbon, pour it over the ice, and fill the glass to the top with club soda.

An old-fashioned is a bourbon drink with lots of fresh fruit: Put about 1/4 teaspoon sugar in the bottom of a double old-fashioned glass, add a few drops of Angostura bitters and 1 teaspoon water, and muddle together. Fill the glass with ice cubes, add 2 ounces of bourbon, and stir. Add a small wedge of lime, a lemon slice, an orange slice, and a maraschino cherry.

GIN AND RUM

Some people go so far as to keep their gin in the refrigerator, for an even more refreshing gin and tonic, the essential summer drink. To make it, use an especially tall highball glass. Fill it with ice cubes, and add 2 ounces of gin. Squeeze in the juice from a generously sized lime wedge, and drop it into the glass. Fill the glass to the top with tonic.

Rum comes in light or dark. Summer drinks require light rum. The mai-tai, for instance, has a tropical flavor: Fill a cocktail shaker with ice cubes, and two double old-fashioned glasses with crushed ice. Combine 3 ounces of light rum, 1 ounce of triple sec, 1 ounce of lime juice, 1 ounce of grenadine syrup, 1 ounce of almond flavored syrup, and 1 teaspoon sugar in the cocktail shaker. Stir it slowly, and allow for some melt. Strain it over the crushed ice in the glasses, and decorate with a maraschino cherry and a pineapple wedge.

A Long Island Iced Tea is delicious. Drink it very slowly, though, and keep adding ice to your glass; it could last you all evening. To make it, fill a cocktail shaker with ice. Add 2 ounce each of light rum, vodka, tequila, and triple sec, and 4 ounces of lemon sour mix. Stir it slowly, and allow for quite a bit of melt. Fill two extra tall highball glasses with ice, and pour the cocktail over it. Add a dash of cola to each glass for the "tea" color, and stir. Decorate with a lemon or lime wedge.

A martini is an all-season cocktail. To make it, fill a cocktail shaker with ice, and add 3 ounces of gin and 1-1/2 ounces of dry vermouth. This is the standard proportion. A "dry" martini could be in the proportion of 5 to 1, or even 8 to 1, gin to vermouth. There are purists who say that the way to make a martini is to pour the gin into the glass, and whisper "vermouth" over it. In any case, stir the mixture slowly, allowing some melt. Strain it into two chilled cocktail glasses, and add a green olive or a twist of lemon peel.

WINE

The subject of fine wine can be intimidating to the uninitiated; few substances are so fraught with history, tradition, sense of place, and outright snobbery. There are whole libraries of wine lore, whole professions built around wine expertise. People devote their entire lives to the appreciation of fine wines, and plan their world travels accordingly.

There seem to be dozens of rules and taboos: you have to have the right wine glass for the right color of wine, you have to drink the right wine at the right time in the meal, and with the right foods. There is a language of wine in which ordinary words like "crisp," "fruity," and "buttery" take on mysterious new meanings. The waiter or wine merchant looks at you funny if you mispronounce the name. You have to spend a fortune to get a really good bottle. It's enough to make you just order a beer and forget about it.

The truth is that while there is a great deal to know about wine, there is no reason to be intimidated. Hard and fast rules are passé, experimentation is the order of the day. If you like it a particular wine with a particular food, then it's good. You're the newly appointed expert. Use whatever glasses you want.

You can get excellent wines at very moderate prices; unless you really are an expert with a finely developed palate, there is absolutely no need to spend more than you are comfortable spending. If the wine merchant with whom you usually deal makes you feel like a pimply teenager at your first dance, and you don't know the dances, find another store to patronize.

We learned everything we know from the wine manager at a fancy liquor store which specializes in fine wines. We displayed our ignorance, asked lots of questions, mispronounced wildly, and were rewarded with enough information to significantly increase our enjoyment while not decreasing our check book by too much.

What we offer here are some general suggestions and ideas. We encourage you to choose whatever wines you want with your menus, and to experiment enough to know what you like. We suggest styles of wines rather than specific vintages from specific vineyards; that part is up to you.

While there is no perfect combination of wine and food, there are certain styles of wine that are likely to work better with certain foods. You can drink red wine with sea food, for example, depending on the red wine. The order in which you drink them doesn't matter, either, although in general it works better to start with a light and dry wine, and move towards a heavier or sweeter one to end the meal.

WINE IN WINTER

With your calamari hors d'oeuvre and your Caesar salad on a cold winter night, try a light, crisp, white wine, such as a Fume Blanc from California, or a Frascati, from the region near Rome. As you experiment, the descriptive words used in the wine business will begin to take on meaning; some Fume Blancs are "crisper" than others, and a Fume Blanc is "lighter" than a Sauvignon Blanc.

The eggplant Parmigiana in that menu could handle an Italian Dolcetto, red with just a touch of sweetness, or a light styled red Beaujolais. The natural choice to end the meal is a little of the Whidbey's Liqueur that you used in your dessert, poured into cordial glasses. Sip it slowly, along with your coffee or cappuccino.

For your Valentine's Feast, start with the bubbly: a sparkling wine such as a dry style Blanc de Noirs, which is the palest of pinks in color. (Only sparkling wines from the Champagne region in France can truly be called champagne).

The lasagna in this dinner provides an excellent opportunity to try a red wine with seafood; a lighter styled red California Zinfandel would go very well. If you would rather stick with a white wine, try a fuller flavored, but still crisp Sauvignon Blanc. You could specify a dry white Graves Sauvignon Blanc, Graves being the region in Bordeaux where Sauvignon Blanc is produced.

Finish it off with cognac. Like champagne, only brandy from the Cognac region of France can be called cognac. Brandy is a distilled wine; it is made from grapes. The grapes grown in the chalky soil of Cognac, and the secret distilling process used there, give cognac a rich and special flavor, wonderfully distinct from your every day brandy. Also like champagne, it is possible to spend your children's college fund on a bottle of cognac, but unnecessary. Choose a moderately priced bottle.

SPRINGTIME WINE

There is an opinion in the wine world that German wines in general don't go well with food. According to our wine mavin, and our tastes, that rule should go out the window with the rest of them. See what you think.

With your brie and green grapes, you want a light, crisp, delicate white wine, such as a dry style German Reisling from the Mosel-Saar-Rewur region. The dryness or sweetness of a wine depends on how ripe the grape was when it was picked. German wine labels designate the dryness of the wine very specifically. To complement the brie and green grapes, look for the words Halb-trocken or Kabinett on the label.

The shrimp and vegetables and pasta would be excellent with a crisper styled California Chardonnay, or a French white burgundy. You could finish this meal off with a sparkling wine; the lemon and tart berry flavors in the dessert could handle a Demi Sec, or even something as sweet as Asti Spumanti.

Gazpacho is Spanish in origin, and its wonderful combination of flavors are made even more wonderful by enjoying a dry Spanish sherry along with it. Fino Sherry is served very cold, and its flavor is delicate, light, and nutty.

Continuing the regional loyalty, but in the new world, try a Pinot Noir from the Willamet Valley in Oregon with your salmon, much of which comes from the Pacific Northwest. If you prefer a white wine with salmon, a white Alsatian would be a good choice. Try another German wine with your fruit and cheese dessert, like an Auslese from the Rhine region.

HIGH SUMMER WINES

The crisp vegetables in your Savory Summer menu would go very well with Vinho Verde, a "spritzy," light, crisp styled white wine from Portugal. Like seafood, chicken no longer requires a white wine, either. Try a red Beaujolais, a lighter styled Zinfandel, or a California Pinot Noir with your pasta salad and chicken breasts. If you prefer white wine with chicken, try a rich, buttery California or Australian Chardonnay.

Try a fruity liqueur with the fruit tart for dessert. Chambord, which comes in the dark, mysterious, round bottle, would be a good choice. Or, you could try some thing generically called a "fruit infusion," and sold as Vin de Glacier. The process of making it involves raspberries at the very peek of their sweet ripeness, and brandy; the result is a sensation, not merely a flavor.

Steam your mussels in Muscadet, a French dry styled white wine, and then have a glass with your hors d'oeuvre. A red wine is still probably the best choice with steak; you couldn't go wrong with a California red Zinfandel.

A Demi Sec sparkling wine would be good with your strawberry short cake, or a little brandy or cognac in a snifter. Brandy has a somewhat lighter flavor than cognac, but cognac tends to be smoother. The smoothest brandies are French Napoleon brandies; Delacour is one example. If you can't find a French Napoleon brandy, and if you like to drink your brandy unadorned out of a snifter, opt for cognac.

AUTUMN WINE

An Italian Pinot Grigio is a dry styled white wine which would complement your steamed scallops and leeks. Try Spätlese, a German Reisling from the Rhine region, with your slightly sweet chicken entrée. It has just a little inherent sweetness. A Reisling from California or Oregon would also be nice.

"Late harvest" grapes make a sweeter wine, which German wine makers label specifically. Look for a sweet, late harvest Auslese from the Rhine region to have with your dessert. It has fruit and apple qualities of its own, which will enhance the flavors of the baked apples.

Go to California for the wines to serve with your rich, decadent rack of lamb dinner: a rich, buttery chardonnay with the rich, buttery bruschetta; a Cabernet Sauvignon or red Bordeaux with the entrée; and, if you can find it, a sweet, late harvest Zinfandel with your sweet, dense chocolate cheesecake. The late harvest designation is sometimes marked on the bottom rim of the bottle; if you don't see it, ask the wine merchant. A late harvest Zinfandel can be hard to find, and a dark, rich port would do just as well.

TOASTING

The custom of drinking to the health of another probably originated around the time the first cup of ale was quaffed by the first relatively civilized beings. While you may not wish to perform this ritual with all of the extravagance it has taken on at various times in history (throwing your glass into the fireplace after downing its contents, for instance, seems an unnecessary flourish), raising your glass to your loved one, and murmuring a few well chosen words is very romantic. Clinking the glasses seems to have originated as a way to complete the ritual aesthetically; with it, all five senses are involved in the enjoyment of the wine.

You could toast each other by quoting Omar Khayyam: "A jug of wine, a loaf of bread — and Thou/ Beside me singing in the wilderness — "

Robert Browning: "Grow old with me! The best is yet to be."

Shakespeare: "May you be merry and lack nothing."

Or Humphry Bogart: "Here's lookin' at you, kid."

You could toast the wine itself, as Horace did: "Let those who drink not, but austerely dine, dry up in law; the Muses smell of wine."

Or, toast in the classic fashion of lovers: "To us."

The most charming toasts will be those you make up yourselves, and there is nothing wrong with merely gazing deeply into each other's eyes as you take your first sip. In any case, here's to romance at home!

Chapter 8

JUST DESSERTS AND OTHER DELIGHTS

*I*t's been one of those really awful weeks. The children had chicken pox. Your helpmate had to be in Omaha (or Pittsburgh, Spokane, Dallas, or Duluth) on business, and couldn't get home on time because of the most terrible storm system in recorded history, which also flooded your basement.

You ran out of milk, bread, apples, macaroni and cheese, and toilet paper, and realized in the check-out line that you were carrying neither cash nor check blanks. The children whimpered in the grocery cart. The rain poured down. The dog threw up six times on the carpet, and needs gastro-intestinal surgery, at approximately the same cost as a cruise around the world on a luxury liner. The transmission on your twelve year old car finally gave out.

Your true love eventually made it home, after spending the last eighteen hours at O'Hare International Airport (or some similar place), and the three days before that trying to put together a business deal that looked great at first, but completely fell apart in the final stages.

Boy, do you two ever need an intimate little dinner at home. You need the quick and easy version. To be more accurate, you need the end result: renewal, rejuvenation, refreshment, romance.

PART OF A DINNER

Part of a romantic dinner is better than none, especially if it's the dessert part, with cappuccino, in front of the fire. If you happen to have some Whidbey's pound cake (Chapter Nine) in your freezer, take it out, and check around for possible toppings. Ice cream in almost any flavor goes well with it. Drizzle on a little chocolate sauce, or any liqueur you like, or both. Sprinkle it with chopped hazelnuts, macadamia nuts, or pecans. Thaw some frozen raspberries with a few drops of liqueur, and pile them on. Add whipped cream, if you have some. Shave slivers off a sweet chocolate bar, and add them.

If you're out of homemade pound cake, maybe you have a frozen cheesecake from your local convenience store; dress it up with a little chocolate sauce, liqueur, fresh or frozen berries, or chopped nuts. If you live in a neighborhood with a nearby delicatessen or bakery, go for something more exotic, like a couple of pieces of chocolate hazelnut torte. Don't forget to light some candles and slip into your silk robe when you get back.

You're more in the mood for an hors d'oeuvre? Make the warm, cheesy bruschetta in Chapter Sixteen, pour a couple of beers, and retire to the bedroom. Fry up some calamari (Chapter Nine), if you have some of the cleaned "tubes" in your freezer. If it's summer and you have lots of fresh vegetables around, make the gazpacho from Chapter Twelve. Chill it as long as you can, or put it in the freezer for about half an hour, and sip it from mugs, sitting on the back porch in the dark.

Maybe you need something more like dinner. Make the Caesar salad in Chapter Nine, using a large head of romaine. Just before serving it, add some thin slices of leftover chicken breast, pork roast, steak, salmon, leg of lamb, duck l'orange, quail with wine, or roast haunch of venison, or a few shrimp from your freezer, thawed, and cooked in one tablespoon olive oil and two tablespoons lemon juice for three minutes.

Make the carrot soup in Chapter Fifteen, and serve it with a sandwich made from French bread, sliced tomato and red onion, a honey mustard or the garlic spread in Chapter Ten, some cheese, and any leftover or prepackaged meat or poultry you happen to have in your refrigerator.

MORSELS

Remember that little box of chocolate truffles you have tucked away? Tonight's the night. Pour a little brandy into your brandy snifters, start the music, and light the candles. If you're out of truffles, maybe you have some chocolate liqueur cups; fill a couple of them with brandy or cognac,

Bailey's, Amaretto, Kahlua, or Schnapps. Drink the liqueur, then eat the cup; it beats tossing a wine glass into the fireplace for a dramatic flourish. Maybe there's a full moon, or lots of stars; open the curtains, and find a good vantage point. Maybe it's still raining; let the sound of it soothe and relax you, you can deal with the flooded basement tomorrow.

Or, let's say it's the hottest night of the summer. Make up a pitcher of lemonade — the frozen concentrate kind, unless you happen to have fifteen lemons on hand — drop a strawberry in each chilled glass, and go sit on the porch, or in the back yard, fanning each other with hand fans. Going back into the air conditioning will be a relief, but there is something romantic about the intense, sultry experience of a hot, hot night.

You could experience it with a Mint Julep: chill two twelve ounce glasses in the freezer for an hour. Remove them from the freezer and put four or five fresh mint leaves in the bottom of each. Add one teaspoon confectioner's sugar and one teaspoon water; muddle together with the mint leaves. Fill each glass with finely crushed ice. Pour in one jigger (an ounce and a half) of bourbon. Stir with a long handled spoon until the glass is frosted, and the ice level is reduced by about an inch and a half. Add more crushed ice to the top, and pour in another jigger of bourbon. Decorate with a sprig of mint dusted with confectioner's sugar. Chill in the freezer for half an hour before serving. Use the time to get into your pajamas; this will be it for today.

Since we're on the subject of drinks that suit the weather, try this on a cold afternoon in November: Make a pot of coffee, not decaffeinated, unless you are ready for a nap. Combine an ounce and half of Irish whiskey and one quarter teaspoon of sugar in the bottom of a large cup or mug (Irish coffee cups are usually glass, with a handle and a short stem). Pour in coffee to within about an inch of the top of the cup. Fill to the top with whipped cream, and grate a little nutmeg or sprinkle a little cocoa mix on top. Drink it through cocktail straws. Have another. Order pizza for supper.

SELF INDULGENCE

Go ahead; declare a self indulgence night. Make use of all the applicable techniques in Chapter Five, or, if you're lucky, let the kids stay with Grandma for a night, or arrange an overnight at a friend's. Lock all the doors, close all the curtains, leave the phone to the answering machine. As soon as the pizza has been delivered, turn off all the lights, except in your bedroom, where you will be dining. Bring in a few beers. Put on your most comfortable old pajamas. Watch a mindless sit-com on TV. Read a trashy novel at the same time. Have two helpings of ice cream. Don't do anything you don't want to do.

Self indulgence means different things to different people. If we just described your nightly routine, then thinking of a meaningful self indulgence night might be a bit more of a challenge. Like your romantic dinners, the point of it is to take a short break from the cares of daily life, and to reconnect with each other on some level (you can at least hold hands while you watch TV, and make eye contact during the commercials), so that you can go forth to face the world again in your usual competent, confident, energetic, and responsible manner, relaxed in your outlook, and renewed in your love life.

EAT TAKEOUT

Think about how much of the work in your life you can delegate to others. With regard to planning your romantic little dinners at home, for instance, where are the good takeout places?

You already know about the pizza place, and probably there are a few Chinese restaurants and a rib joint or two within an easy drive from your house; some might even deliver. There might be a corner cafe ("Rose's Home Cooking," or "Ethel's Kitchen, No Tipping Please") with a previously untapped source of meatloaf sandwiches or banana cream pie. Ethel probably doesn't deliver, but she might pack up her chicken-fried steak with home fries for you on a Saturday night.

What else is out there? Take the time to cruise your neighborhood again, like you did when you were looking for cooking resources. This time, keep an eye out for the interesting little restaurants that might offer take out. As part of your exploration, ask if they deliver, and ask what special things they might be able to offer for a romantic dinner for two. Will the French bakery twist a baguette into a heart shape? Will your favorite rib place tie a velvet ribbon around the polystyrene takeout box? Will the Italian delicatessen supply a tenor?

Make it into an adventure. Eat things you've never eaten before. What is Ethiopian cuisine like, anyway? How is Thai cooking different from other oriental cooking? You've never been in a kosher delicatessen, or tried the deep fried smelt at a Swedish restaurant? And how about that family from Lithuania, Azerbaijan, South Africa, Haiti, Malaysia, or Lebanon, that just opened a restaurant across town? Try a Greek lemon soup, or a Middle Eastern eggplant dip. Try a really hot Indian curry, an authentic Scotch broth, hand made guacamole, sushi. See how many destinations you can reach while never leaving town.

Pick up little samples for each other on your way home from work. Surprise each other with albondiguitas, keftedakia, köttbullar. Bring home kimchee, rumaki, pirozhki, kolace, challah, limpa, paella, mulligatawny soup, zabaglione, or lemon meringue pie. Try every place within range, don't be shy. The fascination of the food is probably in direct proportion to your inability to understand the language of the proprietors.

If you live in or near a large metropolitan area, the possibilities are endless. Even if the nearest city worthy of the name is hundreds of miles away over the mountains or across the desert, you may be surprised at the variety of food you can find if you look. Plan a romantic dinner at home around your findings. If it is logistically possible, you could put together an international feast, or, if your choices or range are limited, do what you can with what you have. Use takeout resources to supplement your own efforts, or don't bother to cook at all, just set the scene and create the mood.

DON'T EAT

After going on and on at great length to make the connection between food and romance, we now feel compelled to point out that exploring the mysteries and delights of the culinary world is not the only way to spice up your relationship. Food, in fact, is not the essential element. Temporary freedom from your children is the essential element.

A desire to enjoy your daily life, an ability to maintain a sense of humor about it and a spirit of adventure about its possibilities, a willingness to take a few risks as it goes along, an ongoing pleasure in each other's company — all of these have applications beyond the dining table. While a romantic dinner together provides a built-in, natural, and easy vehicle in which to renew your romance (sort of like your dad's Buick parked on a dark side street in your younger days), it is not the only way.

Having practiced the parental techniques that allow you to have some time together, you can use the time in any way you please. Think about what your relationship needs. How well do you know each other? What intrigues you about each other? What surprises still lurk, hidden and undiscovered? What activities, besides eating and sex, help you feel connected to each other?

PLAY MUSIC

If you each play an instrument, play together. If neither of you plays anything but the stereo, take up the recorder or ukelele together; there are books written for children about these and other relatively simple instruments, which allow even the musically impaired to learn and enjoy.

If one of you has great musical talent and the other, well, doesn't, you can still find a way to play together. A little tolerance and encouragement on the part of the gifted one, and a little risk-taking and practice on the part of the talentless one, can result in a lot of fun, and a deepening of intimacy.

If the musician normally plays first viola for the New York Philharmonic, or the organ for the Mormon Tabernacle choir, he or she could switch to another instrument or genre to help level the field while playing together. The non-musician could keep rhythm with a percussion instrument, sing a few doo-be-doos in the background, or breathe rhythmically through a harmonica. Music is pretty forgiving to the talentless but enthusiastic.

If instruments don't interest you, sing together. Sing old folk songs, hymns, or rock and roll. Sing along with the radio or TV. Sing opera, lullabies, nonsense, and love songs. Sing loud. Sing in the shower. Make up verses. There is no one who can't sing, just those who don't.

The point, of course, is not to achieve recording-studio quality with your spouse in your living room; the point is to connect with each other and have fun doing it. Music is almost as natural a vehicle for this as eating, and it is one that has been largely lost to the technology and fast pace of the last half of the twentieth century. In earlier ages, an entire courtship might be conducted by means of a piano and a violin, or a guitar and a balcony, or a flute, a harp, a sweet voice, a duet on the porch swing.

DANCE

The idea of taking a class in ballroom dancing as a way to recharge a marriage is nothing new. We recommend the do-it-yourself version, though, for the same reasons we recommend a romantic dinner at home rather than at a restaurant: you are undistracted by others, you can tailor the experience to your own tastes and time frame, and, should you find your romance rekindled right there on the dance floor, you don't have far to go to take advantage of the opportunity.

Instruction books that show two sets of foot prints (frequently, two tiny little circles and two little triangles, paired with two large boot-sole shapes), with dotted lines, arrows, and black and white photographs, are available at the public library. Choose your dance music according to your tastes, and dance 'til dawn in your lover's arms.

READ ALOUD

Reading aloud is another lost method of intimate interaction. The subject matter is completely immaterial; whether you're reading a romance novel or a philosophical treatise, snuggle up on the couch, and enjoy the sound of your true love's voice. Take turns, and stop whenever you like for questions, laughter, or discussion.

Read Agatha Christy, Rex Stout, Dashiel Hammet, Dorothy L. Sayers, and Edgar Allen Poe. Read Wordsworth, Shelley, Keats, Byron, and Coleridge. Read Walt Whitman and Rober Frost. Read Kafka. Read Hemingway. Read plays, short stories, history, memoir, and biography. Read new best sellers, and the writings of the ancients.

Make a project of reading all of Shakespeare's love sonnets to each other, or the love scenes from his plays. Perform tableaux, a popular form of entertainment in Victorian times, involving sets, costumes, grand music, and dramatic readings from the classics. Yours could be greatly modified versions, involving comical readings from Garrison Keillor, for example, with a tape of banjo music in the background.

The object is not to fill in the gaps in your literary education, to expand your literary horizons, or even to increase your enjoyment of what you read, although all of those things are likely to happen, and so much the better. The object is to find a way to be close to each other, sharing something from which the rest of the world is excluded.

PLAN THE TRIP OF A LIFETIME

Travel, at least at the level on which you may wish to experience it, may be about as likely as a voyage on the Starship Enterprise. Remember, though, that the entire itinerary of the Enterprise takes place in the imagination. Get out your atlas, and plan the trip you would most like to take.

Maybe it's a cruise around Cape Horn in your own sailing vessel. Maybe you've always been fascinated by the Al-Can Highway, or the Orient Express. You may have a life-time goal of visiting every National Park, or every Major League ball park, in North America, or every site of Arthurian archeological research in England, or every active volcano in the world. Maybe you'd love an October car trip to Nova Scotia, followed by a drive west along the Great Lakes, ending up on the rugged North Shore of Lake Superior in time for its season of winter storms.

As you plan your itinerary, look for the side trips, the out of the way places, the historical or geological oddities. Look for the *Country Inns and Back Roads,* which is the title of a series of annually updated books put out by Berkshire Traveller Press, covering bed and breakfasts, small hotels, and music festivals in North America, England and Ireland, Europe, and the Caribbean, among other things in other places.

Maybe you'll actually take the trip some day, after the children move out and you retire. For now, mark up your maps and pack your imaginary suitcases, and do your best to picture each other wearing explorer hats and waving from the top of the Pyramid of Kukulcan at Chichen Itza.

PRACTICE MASSAGE

If you have ever experienced a professional massage done by an expert, you know how soothing and utterly relaxing it is. Many books describing the basic techniques are available, often at the same stores that sell various oils and lotions, and tapes of the ocean or New Age music to play in the back ground. Practice on each other. You may lack the expertise provided by a formal training in massage, but you'll make up for it with your intimate knowledge of your true love's ticklish places (which, by the way, you should avoid during the massage).

Try to make it a non-verbal experience, and try to take turns, though the first recipient may have a hard time with his or her responsibility to reciprocate. The purpose, once again, is to connect with each other. The experience should be soothing and relaxing, comforting and pleasant. A massage is not meant as foreplay, although, as with any of your other efforts to spend romantic time together, one never knows what might happen at the end of the evening.

THE GREAT ADVENTURE

Marriage is the great adventure. No other life endeavor can affect your daily happiness and peace of mind to quite such an extent. No other life enterprise requires such vast skills, or yields such deep rewards. Certainly your children are part of the adventure, but, with any luck, they will grow up and move out while you still have half of your married life ahead of you. We hope we have provided a starting place, and only a starting place, in your search for the romance in your life.

Chapter 9

Part two: THE MENUS

BABY, IT'S COLD OUT THERE

Crispy Calamari

Caesar Salad

French Bread

Eggplant Parmigiana

*Whidbey's Pound Cake
with Whipped Cream*

*Manhattan Cocktail (see recipe, page 62),
or California Fume Blanc, or Frascati*

*Italian Dolcetto
or light Beaujolais*

*Whidbey's Liqueur and Coffee
or Cappuccino*

*T*his is a great menu any time of the year, but there is something about melted mozzarella and tomato sauce that warms even the coldest day. If you have a fireplace, set a table for two in front of the fire; otherwise, find another romantic niche in your house, someplace where you don't usually eat. The red checkered tablecloth and the candle in the old chianti bottle would set the scene nicely. Plain white plates and white napkins would be perfect. You could add an arrangement of purple, mauve, yellow, and white statice in a pottery pitcher.

INGREDIENTS AND PLANNING

Check each recipe; make a list of the ingredients you don't have on hand. Check your liquor cabinet and wine cellar. Don't forget a stop at the liquor store if necessary.

Purchase about 1 pound of fresh, whole calamari (8 to 10 squid). If your butcher or fish store stocks the frozen calamari "tubes," you may need to call ahead to make sure the amount you need is ready for you. Thaw them in the refrigerator for several hours.

Make a run through the produce department for a small head of romaine lettuce, and an eggplant weighing about a pound; look for one that is firm, shiny, and unblemished.

If you opt not to make your own bread today, and have none in your freezer, pick up a French bread baguette.

Likewise for dessert; store-bought pound cake is not as good as yours would be, but there is no need to quibble over details. Buy a dessert if you don't have time to make one.

Your last stop will be the flower store. Statice in a variety of colors is usually inexpensive and easy to find. Look for tall stems, which have not begun to brown around the edges. By the way, statice dries nicely; you can simply dry it standing upright in its vase, and use it indefinitely in dried flower arrangements.

Make your musical selections for the evening. Let Luciano Pavarotti entertain you tonight, with either opera or folk songs. Any light Italian opera would be nice, or Vivaldi's Four Seasons, or Boccherini's cello concerto.

TO DO AHEAD

If you are making bread today, start it early. There is nothing difficult about our French bread recipe, and the dough-contact time is not great, but yeast operates on its own schedule. Make the pound cake early in the day, too; you can do it while the bread dough is rising.

No doubt you have a fragrant stack of table linens carefully folded and ready to use in a drawer in your dining room; just check to make sure the tablecloth and napkins you want for tonight are there, and not somewhere in the pile of ironing in your laundry room.

Take time to arrange the flowers as soon as you get them.

You can clean and slice the calamari ahead of time, and refrigerate it until you are ready to cook it.

Make the tomato sauce for the Eggplant Parmigiana late in the afternoon; simmering on a low flame for several hours enhances the flavor. Make sure the flame is very low, and don't forget to stir it occasionally. In fact, you can prepare the whole dish ahead of time. Follow the recipe right up to the baking step, and refrigerate it until about an hour before you will want to eat it. Let it sit out for half an hour before putting the dish in the hot oven.

You can go ahead and bake the eggplant Parmigiana early, too, if you want to. It reheats very well in the microwave, on a medium-high or reheat setting, for about five minutes, or in a 300 degree oven for about fifteen minutes. The exact reheat time for either oven or microwave will depend on how cold the dish was when it went in.

Toast the croutons and mix the dressing for the salad. Wash and refrigerate the romaine. Combine the salad just before serving it.

TASKS FOR CHILDREN

Employ your three to six year old's skills and abilities to pour water and sprinkle yeast, measure and count cups of flour, help knead bread dough, and help shape the baguettes. Some in this age group are especially fond of the job of sprinkling flour onto the bread board during the kneading and shaping process, and they can also prepare the baking pans by sprinkling them with cornmeal.

They are skilled flour sifters, and can stand on a chair next to the mixer and scrape the sides of the bowl with a rubber scraper. They can add ingredients and count eggs. Give a preschooler the job of washing, drying and tearing the romaine, but keep your eye on the process. Give one a long handled spoon to stir the tomato sauce as it cooks, and don't leave out the important cheese sprinkling assignment.

In addition to all that, ask your six to nine year old apprentice to turn on the oven, start mixing the bread dough with a wooden spoon, prepare the cake pans by lining them with foil and buttering them, break the eggs and add them to the cake batter along with the rest of the ingredients, cut bread into squares for croutons, open cans and pour the contents into the pan, and grate cheese. An adventurous one might want to dip the calamari rings into the egg mixture and the bread crumb mixture before frying.

Unless you enjoy the creative experience of setting your romantic table, assign it to a child in this age group, after a brief lesson in handling stemware.

A nine to twelve year old could practically prepare the entire menu. Ask one to mix the bread dough and the cake batter, to punch down the dough, to shape the loaves, slash them after they have risen, and be responsible for baking them. Ask one to start the tomato sauce, slice and salt the eggplant, prepare the salad dressing, and maybe even clean the calamari.

SHARING THE WORK

At the appropriate time,

COOK A	COOK B
fries the calamari	serves the cocktails or wine
boils water for spaghetti	lights the candles
warms the bread	prepares the salad
drains spaghetti	pours wine
	serves eggplant Parmigiana
clears the table	makes coffee
whips the cream	cuts the cake

CRISPY CALAMARI

Calamari is the Italian word for squid. If you are unable to find fresh squid, check with the butchers in a large supermarket. They sometimes stock frozen "tubes," cleaned squid without tentacles, which work fine in this recipe, although many calamari lovers cherish the tentacles. Once they are cooked, dip the crispy calamari rings in a tangy sauce, such as Lingham's Chillie Sauce or Tiger Sauce, both of which are made from sugar, hot red chillies, vinegar, and spices.

8 to 10 whole squid (about one pound)
2 cups vegetable oil
1 egg, slightly beaten
1/4 cup milk
1-1/2 cups dry unseasoned bread crumbs
Salt and pepper to taste

Place the squid in a colander, and rinse with cold water. Taking them one at a time, prepare them as follows: cut off the tentacles, intact, just above the eyes, and set aside. Cut off the eye section, and discard. Holding the tube in one hand, pull from the top to remove the long, thin, clear cartilage (called the pen); discard it. Holding the tube in one hand, gently pull on the fin structure towards the tail end. Continue to pull gently until the speckled outer membrane comes off, leaving the smooth, grayish tube. Cut off about 1/4-inch of the tube at the tail end. Holding the tube under running cold water, and using a motion like milking a cow, squeeze to remove the viscera. Make sure all viscera are removed, and rinse the tubes well. Leave the tentacles whole. Cut the tubes into 1/2-inch rings. Rinse again in a colander under cold water, and pat dry with paper towels.

Heat the oil until very hot in a large kettle suitable for deep frying. (The oil is hot enough when a drop of water sizzles in it). Combine the egg and the milk in a small bowl; combine the bread crumbs, salt, and pepper on a plate. Dredge each ring and the tentacles first in the egg mixture, then in the bread crumb mixture, and drop into the hot oil. Cook until golden brown and crispy, two to three minutes. Remove with a slotted spoon and drain on paper towels.

To serve, arrange the calamari on a plate, garnish with a lemon wedge, and dip in Lingham's Chillie Sauce, Tiger Sauce, or something similar.

CAESAR SALAD

This is an eggless version, with all the flavor and spirit you'd expect of a Caesar Salad.

Freshly ground black pepper to taste
3 cloves garlic, crushed
1 teaspoon anchovy paste
1/4 teaspoon salt
3 tablespoons extra virgin olive oil
2 tablespoons white wine vinegar
1 tablespoon lemon juice
1/4 teaspoon dry mustard
1 small head of romaine, washed, leaves torn into pieces
Freshly grated Parmesan cheese to taste
1 cup croutons
*(1-inch squares of French bread toasted in a skillet on the stove top
with 1 tablespoon olive oil and 1 clove chopped garlic)*

Combine pepper, garlic, anchovy paste, and salt in the bottom of a large wooden salad bowl. Combine olive oil, vinegar, lemon juice, and mustard, add to salad bowl, mix well. Add romaine, toss with dressing. Add Parmesan cheese, toss again. Add croutons, toss again.

FRENCH BREAD

This recipe makes six baguettes, which freeze very well. It is delicious and easy.

3 cups warm (105° - 115° f) water
2 tablespoons (2 packets) active dry yeast
4 teaspoons coarse kosher salt
8 cups unbleached white flour

Pour the water into a large bread bowl, sprinkle the yeast on top, and set in a warm place for about 10 minutes to dissolve. Add the salt and 7 cups of the flour, mixing with a wooden spoon.

Turn the dough out onto a bread board lightly floured with some of the remaining cup of flour. Knead the dough gently and firmly, turning and folding, and adding flour underneath as needed to prevent sticking, for about 10 minutes. When the dough is smooth and no longer sticky, form it into a ball.

Lightly oil your bread bowl with vegetable oil, and return the dough to it, turning the ball of dough once or twice, so that all of it is thinly coated with oil. Cover the bowl with a dampened dish towel, and set it in a warm place. Allow the dough to rise for about an hour, until it has doubled in bulk. Punch it down firmly, knead it briefly in the bowl, form it into a ball, cover it, and let it rise until double again.

Punch the dough down again, turn it out onto your bread board, and knead it briefly. Using a pastry scraper or knife, divide the dough in half, and each half into thirds. Form each piece into a ball. Prepare two 12x15x1-inch baking sheets by sprinkling them lightly with corn meal.

Shape each ball as follows: flatten it into an oval; mark a line down the middle with the side of your hand; fold the dough along the line; roll it into a cylinder. Continue rolling the cylinder back and forth on the bread board until it is as long as the baking pan (15-inches), thin, and tapered at the ends. Place three baguettes lengthwise on each baking pan.

Cover the pans, and let the baguettes rise until they have doubled in bulk, about an hour. Preheat the oven to 400 degrees. When the baguettes have doubled, make four shallow, diagonal slashes in each one. Bake 25 minutes, until they are golden brown and sound hollow when tapped. Turn the pans and change racks half way through the baking.

Cool completely on racks. To freeze, wrap each baguette separately, first in plastic wrap, then in tin foil.

EGGPLANT PARMIGIANA

Eggplant is a remarkable vegetable; in this dish, it hardly seems like a vegetable at all. This recipe would serve four to six at a dinner party; save your leftovers for tomorrow, or freeze them for another time.

1 eggplant, about 1 pound, cut into 1/2-inch slices,
salted generously, placed in a colander

olive oil (for frying the eggplant slices)
3 tablespoons olive oil (for sauce)
1 shallot, chopped
1 leek, white part only, chopped
2 cloves garlic, chopped
1 (28 ounce) can crushed tomatoes
1 (8 ounce) can tomato sauce
1 (6 ounce) can tomato paste
1/2 cup dry red wine
1/2 cup snipped fresh parsley
1 teaspoon dried basil
1 teaspoon dried oregano
1/2 teaspoon fennel seed, crushed
Salt and freshly ground black pepper to taste
1/4 cup freshly grated Parmesan cheese
1 cup grated Mozzarella cheese
About 8 ounces spaghetti or linguini, cooked

Set the salted eggplant slices aside for 30 minutes. Heat 3 tablespoons olive oil in a 4-1/2 quart kettle. Add the shallot, leek, and garlic, sauté until tender, about 5 minutes. Add the crushed tomatoes, tomato sauce, tomato paste, and red wine. Let it come to a boil, and reduce the heat. Add parsley, basil, oregano, fennel, salt and pepper. Simmer slowly for about 30 minutes, stirring occasionally. Preheat the oven to 400 degrees.

Carefully rinse the eggplant slices under cold running water, and pat them dry with a paper towel. Measure 2 tablespoons olive oil into a large frying pan, heat it, and add a single layer of eggplant slices. Fry until lightly browned on both sides, without adding any more oil. Drain on paper towels. Measure another 2 tablespoons olive oil into the pan, and repeat, until all the eggplant slices are fried.

Spread 1/2 cup of the sauce into the bottom of a 12-inch, round, straight-sided baking dish. Arrange a single layer of eggplant over the sauce, sprinkle with about 1/3 of the Parmesan cheese and 1/3 of the mozzarella. Add half of the remaining sauce, then repeat the layering process. Repeat again with the rest of the sauce, ending with the last of the mozzarella. Bake for 30 minutes; let stand for 10 minutes before serving. Serve with cooked spaghetti.

WHIDBEY'S POUND CAKE

Whidbey's is a liqueur made from loganberries, grown on the West Coast, and similar in flavor and color to raspberries. Another fruit based liqueur, such as Grand Marnier or Cherry Heering, could be used instead to flavor the pound cake. Cake flour is finer than all purpose flour; look for it packaged in 2-pound boxes in the baking supplies section of a large grocery store. This recipe could easily be halved, but we offer the big version because it freezes well, and is endlessly versatile. It could serve twelve for a dinner party or buffet.

1-1/2 cups butter, softened

3 cups sugar

8 eggs

4 cups sifted cake flour

1 tablespoon baking powder

1/2 teaspoon salt

1/2 teaspoon freshly grated nutmeg

3 tablespoons Whidbey's liqueur

1/2 cup whipping cream, whipped with 1 tablespoon sugar
and 1 teaspoon Whidbey's liqueur

Preheat oven to 325 degrees. Line two 4-1/2x8-inch loaf pans with tin foil, letting it extend over the ends of the pans so you can lift the cakes out. Butter generously.

Cream the butter and sugar until light in color. Add the eggs one at a time, beating well each time. Sift the flour before measuring, and sift again with the baking powder, nutmeg and salt. Add about a third of this mixture at a time, alternating with a third of the liqueur, and beating well after each addition.

Bake for one hour, until a toothpick inserted in center comes out clean. Cool for 30 minutes on a rack, remove from pans, and cool completely. To serve, cut into 1/2-inch slices, and top each slice with a generous dollop of whipped cream. If you like, drizzle it with a little more of the liqueur. For variations, add blueberries, strawberries, raspberries, peach slices, or any other seasonal fruit, add ice cream, add chopped hazelnuts, pecans, or walnuts, or add chocolate sauce, slivers cut from a chocolate bar, or sprinkles of cocoa mix.

To freeze, cut each cake into thirds, and wrap each piece first in plastic wrap, then in tin foil. Thaw at room temperature for several hours.

SERVING YOUR WINTER SUPPER

Tuck a "snowflake" cut from white paper under each napkin, to remind you of the cold outside.

Serve your calamari on small plates, with a lemon wedge, and a tangy dipping sauce, like Lingham's Chillie Sauce or Tiger Sauce. Drink your Manhattan or light white wine (Fume Blanc or Fruscati) with it. Move on to your salad, served from a big wooden salad bowl onto large salad plates.

Serve your bread, warmed and covered with a napkin in a bread basket, with the salad, but leave it on the table when you serve the entrée. Nothing is better than French bread for mopping up tomato sauce.

Pour the red wine (Dolcetto or light Beaujolais) into big, bowl-shaped wine glasses. Serve the Eggplant Parmigiana from the kitchen. If you are serving it with spaghetti or linguini, serve that up in the kitchen, too, and spoon some sauce over it. Put a chunk of whole Parmesan cheese and a small grater on the table.

Make the coffee or cappuccino, clear the table, whip the cream, and serve dessert. Pour a little Whidbey's liqueur into cordial glasses. Enjoy!

Chapter 10

VALENTINE'S FEAST

Herb Stuffed Mushrooms and Cherry Tomatoes

*Radicchio Salad
with Honey Mustard Dressing*

Garlic Bread

Seafood Lasagna

Lacy Chocolate Hearts

Dry Blanc de Noirs

*California Zinfandel
or Graves Sauvignon Blanc*

Coffee and Cognac

Get out your fine china plates and crystal champagne flutes for this dinner, and set the table with a lacy white tablecloth and napkins. Use your most elaborate candle holders; surround yourself with as many candles as you can. Long stemmed red roses are traditional for Valentine's Day, and a fine tradition it is, too. Put them in a tall, elegant vase.

INGREDIENTS AND PLANNING

Check each recipe; make a list of the ingredients you don't have on hand. Check your liquor cabinet and wine cellar. Don't forget a stop at the liquor store if necessary.

Buy eight ounces each of fresh shrimp and scallops, and an eight ounce filet of sole. If you will be using frozen fish and seafood, let it thaw in your refrigerator for several hours.

In the produce department, choose the biggest, smoothest, nicest, stuffable mushrooms you can find. If your store lets you hand pick the cherry tomatoes, look for the biggest, reddest ones. Choose a small head of radicchio, one with no discoloration on the outer leaves.Choose a bunch of basil that looks fresh and crisp, not wilted or discolored. Buy enough so that it will make about a cup when the stems are removed and the leaves are torn apart.

If you have no French bread in your freezer, and don't have time to make it (from the recipe in Chapter Nine), pick up a baguette at a bakery.

Buy the cheeses; if you can get them already grated, so much the better. By the way, you can freeze mozzarella and provolone cheese. We buy 5 pound bags of grated, mixed mozzarella and provolone. We keep it frozen, and pull off the amount we need, not only for this lasagna, but for pizza, Eggplant Parmigiana, or Bruschetta.

Long stemmed red roses are very popular around Valentine's Day, so order yours well ahead. Pick them up on the day of your dinner.

Select your music. Play whatever music has significance for you — pieces played at your wedding, for instance. If your tastes have changed over the years, allow us to suggest Pachelbel's Kanon, Grieg's Piano Concerto in A minor, Beethoven's Emperor Concerto, and Vladimir Horowitz, The Last Recording.

TO DO AHEAD

Start by making the Chocolate Hearts. The recipe from which ours is adapted comes from a 1925 booklet put out by the Baker Company. In an age when many cooks still relied on wood stoves, and a large part of the skill of baking had to do with knowing how much of what kinds of wood to use to make the oven hotter or cooler, the recipe cautions that its success depends entirely on the oven temperature, which should be "very moderate." Luckily, we can simply turn the dial to 300 degrees, and pretty much count on the desired results. Do it early in the day, though, before you have baked anything else at a hotter temperature.

Make the seafood lasagna ahead of time, too. Follow the recipe up to the baking step, and refrigerate until about an hour and a half before you want to eat it. Let it sit out for about half an hour before putting the dish into the hot oven.

You can bake it early, too, if you want to. Like other dishes that include a tomato sauce, it benefits from sitting around for a while, and reheats very well. Cool it after baking, and then refrigerate until twenty to thirty minutes before you want to eat it. Let it sit out for about 15 minutes, then reheat in individual portions in the microwave, on a medium or reheat setting for about three minutes, or reheat the whole pan for fifteen minutes in a 300 degree oven.

Roast the head of garlic for the garlic bread. If you are baking your lasagna early, you can roast the garlic at the same time, creating a wonderful combination of smells.

Chances are your lacy white tablecloth and napkins don't get a lot of use these days. Pull them carefully from the bottom of your linen drawer, shake out the wrinkles, and let them air. Check to see if they need ironing.

Arrange the roses as soon as you get them home. Clip off about one-fourth of an inch from the bottom of each stem, at an angle, before you put them in water, and they will last longer.

Prepare the stuffing for the hors d'oeuvre; clean, prepare, and stuff the mushrooms and cherry tomatoes, and put them in a greased pie tin, ready for their brief moment under the broiler.

Mix the salad dressing, and wash and tear the radicchio. Use the delicate red leaf part, and discard most of the tougher, white stem part. Taste the leaves, and if the flavor is very strong, you could add a little green or red leaf lettuce. The dressing is quite sweet, though, and does remarkable things to the slightly bitter radicchio.

Make sure your bread is ready to be sliced, and your butter is soft.

TASKS FOR CHILDREN

Definitely involve your preschooler in making the chocolate hearts. Three to six year olds will be fascinated by the process; the way the chocolate seems to disappear into the sugar, and then reappears again when you add the egg whites; the way the dough looks and feels as you form it into a paste and then roll it out; and the way the hearts pop up to about twice their original height as they bake. They will also be fascinated by the end product; no need to be concerned about left-overs with this one.

A preschooler could also be enlisted as sauce stirrer, noodle dryer, and cheese sprinkler, as a mushroom washer and tomato counter, and as a dressing shaker. Ask one to wash and tear up the basil leaves, and to rinse and dry the seafood and fish.

An older child, in the six to nine year old group, could also chop up the seafood, grate the cheeses, arrange the lasagna noodles in the pan, and spoon in the sauce. Ask one to measure herbs, stuff the mushrooms, and poke some of the herb stuffing into those tiny little spaces in the cherry tomatoes. Ask one to mix the salad dressing, and teach one how to separate the leaves of radicchio and prepare them for the salad. Kids in this age group will also be able to roll out the dough for the chocolate hearts, cut them with a cookie cutter, and transfer them to a baking sheet; the dough handles easily when sprinkled with granulated sugar.

If you trust your six to nine year old with your fine china and crystal, and if you don't cherish the task for yourself, have one set the Valentine's table.

A nine to twelve year old could be given complete responsibility for the chocolate hearts, the herb stuffing, the salad, roasting the garlic, and preparing it for the bread. Demonstrate how to gently separate the cloves, and scrape out the garlic. Ask your child to complete that process, combine it with the butter, and spread it on the bread.

Hand the lasagna recipe to your young master chef, and be available to answer questions and provide manual labor as needed (draining the noodles, for instance). Getting all the components of lasagna in the right place at the right time and in the proper condition can be a challenge. Because it is much like planning a meal, it provides an excellent training for an aspiring cook. You could help by teaching your child to lay out all the ingredients ahead of time, and to arrange them in the groups in which they will be combined.

SHARING THE WORK

At the appropriate time,

COOK A	COOK B
opens the sparkling wine	broils the hors d'oeuvre
	lights candles
prepares salad	prepares garlic bread
serves lasagna	pours wine
makes coffee	clears the table
serves dessert	pours cognac

HERB STUFFED MUSHROOMS AND CHERRY TOMATOES

The white mushrooms and red cherry tomatoes carry out the Valentine's Day theme; stuffing them with herbs is delicious and easy.

4 very large white mushrooms, washed, stems removed
(reserve 2 of the stems)
8 cherry tomatoes, washed
1 tablespoon olive oil
2 of the reserved mushroom stems, chopped
1 tablespoon chopped green onions or chives, chopped
1 tablespoon chopped fresh parsley
1 teaspoon dried basil
1 teaspoon dried oregano
1/2 teaspoon dried rosemary, crumbled
1 tablespoon dry seasoned bread crumbs
Salt and freshly ground black pepper to taste
1 tablespoon freshly grated Parmesan cheese

Preheat broiler. Heat the oil in a small frying pan. Add the mushroom stems, and chives or scallions; cook until tender, about 2 minutes.

Add parsley, basil, oregano, and rosemary; cook, stirring, for another minute. Add bread crumbs, and salt and pepper. Stir, and remove from the heat. Add parmesan cheese and mix well.

Fill the mushroom caps with the mixture. Use a small, sharp knife to cut a small cone out of the top of the cherry tomatoes, fill that with the herb mixture. Put mushrooms and tomatoes in a greased pie tin, broil 3 minutes.

Remove to a serving plate, and cool slightly before serving.

RADICCHIO SALAD WITH HONEY MUSTARD DRESSING

The red of the radicchio makes it a nice valentine. The honey in the dressing sweetens its slight bitterness, but you can add some red or green leaf lettuce if the flavor is too strong.

2 tablespoons Dijon style mustard
2 tablespoons walnut oil
1 tablespoon honey
1 small head of radicchio, torn apart, washed, and dried

Mix the mustard, oil, and honey together in a small bowl until they are well blended and smooth. Arrange the radicchio leaves on salad plates. Drizzle the dressing over them. Serve at once.

GARLIC BREAD

This is a true garlic lover's version. Though you roast a whole head of garlic, you only use part of it at a time. Leave the rest whole and unpealed, and store it in a tightly sealed plastic bag in your refrigerator; you can use some whenever you have a need for crushed garlic. Use home-made French bread from Chapter Nine, or buy a baguette from a bakery.

1 whole head of garlic
1 tablespoon butter, softened
8 slices French bread, about 1/2-inch thick,
slightly warmed

Leave the head of garlic whole and unpealed. Preheat the oven to 350 degrees, and roast the garlic in a small pie tin or cake pan for one hour. Let it cool until it can be handled. Put the softened butter in a small dish. Gently peal off one of the outer cloves of garlic. Gently pull apart the peeling on it, and scrape out the garlic with a butter knife; it will have the consistency of soft butter. Add the garlic to the butter in the dish. Continue with additional cloves of garlic until you have an amount equal to the amount of butter. Mix well. Spread the mixture on the slices of French bread; serve at once.

SEAFOOD LASAGNA

This makes a full pan of lasagna, which is a lot for dinner for two. You won't regret it, though. Eat the leftovers for lunch on Sunday, or for dinner during the week, or freeze them for another night. The flavors get deeper and richer when it is reheated. This recipe could serve twelve at a dinner party. Double concentrated tomato paste comes in a tube; look for it with the canned tomato products in a large grocery store, or in a specialty shop.

2 tablespoons olive oil
1 leek, white part only, chopped
1 shallot, chopped
1 (28 ounce) can crushed tomatoes
1 tablespoon double concentrated tomato paste
1 cup loosely packed fresh basil leaves, washed and torn into pieces
Salt and freshly ground black pepper to taste
8 ounces shrimp,
washed, shelled, deveined, and coarsely chopped
8 ounces bay scallops, rinsed and halved
8 ounces sole filet, rinsed and cut into 1/2-inch pieces
2 cups Mozzarella cheese, shredded
1 cup Provolone cheese, shredded
12 plain or spinach lasagna noodles,
cooked, drained, and rinsed

Heat the olive oil in a large frying pan. Add the leek and shallot, sauté until tender, about 3 minutes. Add tomatoes and tomato paste, 1/4 cup of the basil, and the salt and pepper. Cook slowly, uncovered, until the sauce has thickened a little, about 20 minutes. Add the shrimp, scallops, and sole, cook over very low heat for another 10 minutes. Combine the cheeses. Preheat the oven to 350 degrees.

Spread about 1/2 cup of the sauce over the bottom of a 9x13-inch lasagna pan. Arrange a single layer of 4 lasagna noodles on top of the sauce. Spoon 1/3 of the remaining sauce over the noodles. Sprinkle with 1/3 of the remaining basil, and 1/3 of the combined cheeses. Repeat twice more, ending with the cheese.

Bake for 45 to 50 minutes, until the top is browned, and the sauce is bubbling around the edges. Let it sit for about 10 minutes before cutting.

LACY CHOCOLATE HEARTS

This recipe is adapted from one that appeared in a 1925 booklet put out by the Baker Company. A primary purpose of the booklet seems to have been to convince cooks and homemakers of the wholesome, nutritional, and medicinal qualities of chocolate. Don't worry, though, these little hearts are pure fluff.

3 ounces unsweetened chocolate
3-3/4 cups powdered sugar
2 egg whites
1 teaspoon vanilla
Granulated sugar

Preheat the oven to 300 degrees. Lightly grease two baking sheets. In a small bowl or double boiler, melt the chocolate over gently boiling water. Remove it from the heat, and transfer it to a mixing bowl. Sift the confectioner's sugar into the chocolate in the bowl, mix with a wooden spoon. As you do this, the chocolate will seem to disappear into the sugar, but it will reappear when you add the egg whites.

Add the egg whites one at a time, and stir to form a stiff but pliable paste. The original recipe is tricky at this point, calling for three egg whites or less. Be careful if your eggs are very large; too much egg white will make the mixture too runny, and you will have to add more confectioner's sugar to get the right consistency. Add the vanilla, and use your hands to mix thoroughly.

Sprinkle a bread board generously with granulated sugar. Break off a piece of the chocolate paste about the size of a plum, flatten it slightly on the board, sprinkle it with granulated sugar, and roll it out with a rolling pin to about 1/4-inch thick. Cut with a 4-inch heart shaped cookie cutter. Transfer the hearts to the lightly greased baking sheet. Sprinkle again with granulated sugar, red if you like. Continue until all the paste is used.

Bake for 15 to 20 minutes. When done, the hearts will feel firm to the touch, like a meringue. Let them sit on the baking sheet for a minute, then transfer them to a rack to cool.

Served them on heart shaped doilies on a plate and eat them like cookies, or stand one up in a dish of ice cream, and drizzle with a liqueur or sprinkle with berries. At Christmas time, use a 4-inch Christmas tree cookie cutter, and sprinkle with green sugar.

Store leftovers in a tightly sealed container or plastic bag, and give them to your children the next day.

SERVING YOUR VALENTINE'S FEAST

Hide a Valentine's candy, or a chocolate kiss, in each napkin.

Arrange your herb stuffed mushrooms and cherry tomatoes on a pink glass serving plate, and set a pink glass salad plate at each place. Pink glass is plentiful at antique stores, and the effect is charming, especially with the pale pink, sparkling, Blanc de Noirs, poured into crystal flutes.

Finish off the sparkling wine with your radicchio salad, then clear the table for your entrée. Serve the garlic bread arranged in a single layer on a white napkin on a silver platter. Pour your wine (red Zinfandel or white Sauvignon Blanc) into stemmed crystal glasses. Serve the lasagna from the kitchen, on your finest china plates.

For dessert, put a heart shaped paper doily on each dessert plate, and overlap two Lacy Chocolate Hearts on top of that. Drink your coffee from fine china cups; they don't have to match your dinner plates, you can try to find special coffee cups at antique stores or gift shops. The proper glassware is important for cognac; use large snifters, hold them in the palm of your hand to warm the cognac, and sip slowly.

Chapter 11

SPRING IS FOR LOVERS

Cracker Bread and Brie
Served with Green Grapes

Green Salad
with Balsamic Vinaigrette Dressing

Focaccia

Linguini
with Shrimp and Garden Vegetables

Lemon Souffle with Fresh Berries

Martini (see recipe, page 63)
or dry German Reisling

California Chardonnay
or French white Burgundy

Coffee and Demi Sec
or Asti Spumanti

*T*he entrée in this menu cooks in about ten minutes, and tastes like an evening walk through the garden. Serve dinner on the porch, if you can, or set your table for two in front of an open window. Use an old floral tablecloth and napkins, and old-fashioned plates. Try to find some heavy, pressed-glass goblets for your wine. Arrange a few tall forsythia branches in a tall vase or bottle, and set them on the floor next to your table. Set a pair of tall, column candles in the middle of the table.

INGREDIENTS AND PLANNING

Check each recipe; make a list of the ingredients you don't have on hand. Check your liquor cabinet and wine cellar. Don't forget a stop at the liquor store if necessary.

Buy about three quarters of a pound of fresh shrimp, medium to large in size. If you will be using frozen shrimp, thaw them in the refrigerator for several hours.

In the dairy section, pick up a small round of brie, and a half-pint of whipping cream.

Look for the plumpest, brightest green grapes you can find in the produce section. You won't need much for your hors d'oeuvre, but you might as well get a couple of pounds for the kids to enjoy. While you're there, hand pick the nicest green beans; they should be crisp, straight, unblemished, and uniform in size. You'll need only about a quarter of a pound for your entrée. Choose a nice, big, bright green pepper, and a red one to match.

If spring is far enough advanced so that you can get fresh blueberries, raspberries, or strawberries in your own garden or from a farmer's market or roadside stand, by all means do so; otherwise, find the best half-pint you can in your grocer's produce department.

If you choose not to make your own pasta today, buy it fresh from a delicatessen if you can. You can probably get your focaccia there, too, if you don't have time to make it. And, while you're there, check out the selection of crackers and cracker bread, if you decide not to make that.

Unless you are lucky enough to have a blooming forsythia in your yard, stop at a florist for a few choice branches. They will last several weeks in a vase with water; use a vase, bottle, or jug that is tall enough to support them.

Think of spring when you select your music. Any works of Mozart would be perfect. Try *Eine kleine Nachtmusik,* or his sonatas for piano and violin in A major and F major.

TO DO AHEAD

If you decide to make your own focaccia, start it fairly early in the day. It only needs to rise once, for about an hour, but it's nice to get it out of the way, and if it's a warm day, you won't want your oven on in the afternoon.

Make the cracker bread early, too, for the same reason. It bakes at the same temperature as the focaccia, so if you make it while the focaccia rises, you will only have to heat the oven once. If you doubt the wisdom of making your own crackers, just try the recipe, and see what you think. It's very simple, and surprisingly delicious.

Make the lemon souffle. It is actually more of a custard than a souffle, and benefits from several hours of chilling.

Now for the pasta. Allow yourself plenty of time, especially if you are new at it, or if you will be relying heavily on the assistance of your children. Once you get the hang of it, it won't actually take you long, but you still want it done well before supper time. Wrap it in plastic wrap until it is time to cook it.

Put the forsythia in water as soon as you get it home.

If your floral tablecloth and napkins really are old, and are made from cotton or linen instead of polyester, they might need ironing to look their best.

Mix the salad dressing; refrigerate.

Clean the berries, and refrigerate.

Take the brie out of the refrigerator, so it can reach room temperature by the time you want to eat it.

Wash the salad greens, prepare the vegetables, and put the salads together on the plates, without the dressing; cover the plates tightly with plastic wrap, and refrigerate.

The shrimp dish lends itself well to what we think of as a Chinese method of preparation. That doesn't necessarily imply the use of a wok, although one would work very well. In stir frying, all of the ingredients are added to a hot pan in quick succession, so you have to have them all cleaned, chopped, minced, measured, combined, and lined up in the right order on your counter before you turn on the burner.

For this dish, you can set things up ahead of time this way: Measure the olive oil into the pan; chop the garlic, measure the red pepper onto it, and leave it in a little pile on one end of the cutting board; prepare the beans and peppers, leave them in a pile next to the garlic pile; clean the shrimp, put them next to the vegetables (if your arrangement will be sitting out for longer than about twenty minutes, refrigerate the shrimp); slice the sundried tomatoes, chop the parsley, and put them together, last in line. When it comes time to cook, the whole thing will go like clockwork.

TASKS FOR CHILDREN

This is a great meal for preschoolers to help cook, because there is lots of sprinkling and kneading. Have one sprinkle yeast, herbs, and the salt on top of the bread. Have one sprinkle sesame seeds into the cracker dough, flour onto the kneading board, and lemon zest into the souffle. Let one help knead bread dough, cracker dough, and pasta dough. Let one practice using a rolling pin, and a cookie cutter; the cracker bread dough is easier to handle than any cookie dough. Making cracker bread together has another advantage. It allows you to teach the valuable lesson that even things that usually come in boxes don't have to.

A six to nine year old apprentice can turn on the oven, and measure ingredients for cracker dough, bread dough, pasta dough, and for the lemon souffle. Kids this age can separate eggs, beat egg whites, use a rolling pin and a cookie cutter effectively, and probably squeeze and grate a lemon. They can be in charge of the mixer operation. Have them wash and slice the greens and vegetables, clean the berries, and, if they are willing, clean the shrimp. They can also make the salad dressing, and set the table, unless you enjoy the task of setting your special table yourself.

Besides all of that, a nine to twelve year old could be given complete responsibility for the crackers, the focaccia, or the lemon souffle, and would not need much help with the pasta. If one is available at the proper time, he or she could cook the shrimp dish. If one is still around at dessert time, he or she could whip the cream.

SHARING THE WORK

At the appropriate time,

COOK A	COOK B
Arranges hors d'oeuvre	Serves cocktails or wine
Lights candles	
Warms bread	Prepares salad
Cooks shrimp dish	Cooks pasta
	Pours wine
Clears the table	Whips cream
Makes coffee	Serves dessert

CRACKER BREAD AND BRIE SERVED WITH GREEN GRAPES

Roquefort cheese is also delicious in combination with the green grapes. If you don't want to make your own crackers, use Bremer's Wafers, Carr's Table Water Crackers, or Valley Lahvosh (heart shaped cracker bread).

1 cup unbleached white flour
1 tablespoon sesame seeds
1/4 teaspoon baking powder
1/4 teaspoon salt
2 tablespoons cold margarine
1/4 cup cold water
4 ounce brie cheese, at room temperature
2 small bunches of green grapes

Combine flour, sesame seeds, baking powder, and salt. Cut in the margarine in small pieces; combine with a pastry blender. Add cold water, knead the mixture into a dough. Form into a ball, wrap in plastic wrap, chill for 30 minutes. Preheat oven to 400 degrees. On a lightly floured board, roll out a little of the dough at a time to about 1/8-inch thick. Cut with a 4-inch heart shaped cookie cutter, transfer to an ungreased baking sheet, bake 15 minutes, until light brown. Cool. Serve spread with the cheese and garnished with the grapes.

GREEN SALAD WITH BALSAMIC VINAIGRETTE DRESSING

Many varieties of hot-honey mustard are available. Each produces a slightly different result, all of which are excellent (at least in our rather extensive experience with hot-honey mustards). A dijon style mustard also works well. Almond oil may be hard to fine, except at a specialty gourmet shop. You can substitute walnut oil, or safflower oil.

3 tablespoons extra virgin olive oil
1 tablespoon almond oil
2 teaspoons balsamic vinegar
2 teaspoons hot-honey mustard
Salt and freshly ground black pepper to taste
6 to 8 large leaves of green leaf lettuce,
washed, dried, and torn apart
1/2 cucumber, thinly sliced
2 large white button mushrooms,
washed and thinly sliced
2 thin slices red onion,
pulled apart into rings

Combine oils, vinegar, mustard, salt and pepper in a small covered container and shake well. Arrange the lettuce and vegetables on plates. Shake the dressing again, pour half over each salad, serve at once.

FOCACCIA

This is an Italian herb bread, round and flat, fragrant and delicious.

1 cup warm water
1 tablespoon (1 packet) active dry yeast
1/4 cup (total) chopped, loosely packed
fresh basil, oregano, and sage,
(or 1 teaspoon each if the herbs are dried)
2 tablespoons olive oil
1 teaspoon salt
1 cup whole wheat flour

2 cup unbleached white flour
1/4 teaspoon coarse kosher salt (optional)

Pour the water into a large bread bowl, sprinkle the yeast on top, and set aside in a warm place to dissolve, about 10 minutes. Add herbs, 1 tablespoon of the olive oil, salt, and whole wheat flour. Mix with a wooden spoon. Add the unbleached flour, continue mixing. Turn the dough out onto a lightly floured board. Knead until all the flour is worked in, and the dough is smooth and no longer sticky. If necessary, add flour as you knead to prevent sticking. Form the dough into a ball.

Lightly oil your bread bowl, return the dough to it, and turn it once or twice, so that all of it is thinly coated with oil. Cover the bowl with a dampened dish towel, set it in a warm place, and let the dough rise until double in bulk, about 1 hour.

Punch the dough down, turn it out onto your bread board, and knead it briefly. Preheat the oven to 400 degrees. Spread about half of the remaining tablespoon of olive oil over the bottom of a 13-inch pizza pan.

Flatten the dough with your hands into a round shape, use a floured rolling pin to roll it out to the size of your pan. Place the dough in the pan, and use a fork to prick holes at random all over it, about 2 inches apart. Spread the rest of the olive oil over the top, and, if desired, sprinkle with the coarse salt.

Bake for 25 minutes, until it is golden brown. Cut into pie-shaped pieces to serve.

LINGUINI

Fresh pasta relegates all other pasta to the level of mediocrity. While you can buy excellent fresh pasta at specialty shops or delicatessens, the experience of making your own is worth the effort. It requires some time and muscle, and the right equipment; if you want to try it, invest in a hand pasta machine, which is available at most large department stores. The tricky part of making pasta is learning to recognize the right consistency of the dough. If it is too dry, it won't cohere; if it is too sticky, it won't cut properly. Give yourself a chance to practice. Look for semolina flour in the pasta section of a large grocery store, or at a specialty food shop.

1 cup unbleached white flour
3/4 cup semolina flour
2 eggs
1 tablespoon salt
2 teaspoons olive oil
1 tablespoon water, or less

Mix the flours together in a large bowl. Make a well in the center and break the eggs into it. Add the salt and olive oil. With a fork, begin in the center, where the eggs are, and slowly mix the eggs and flour.

Turn the dough out onto a lightly floured board, and begin kneading. The dough will be firm and difficult to knead. If it is too stiff, add the water, a few drops at a time. If it gets too sticky, work in more flour, a little at a time. Continue to work it until it is smooth and somewhat elastic.

Cover with a dampened dish towel, and let the dough "rest" for about 10 minutes. Use a rolling pin to flatten about 1/4 of the dough at a time into roughly rectangular shapes. Follow the directions that came with your pasta machine to role it and cut it. Keep the dough covered until you are ready to cut it. Wrap the cut pasta in plastic wrap until you are ready to cook it.

To cook, drop it into rapidly boiling water. Remember that fresh pasta cooks in about 30 seconds; it is done when it rises to the top of the boiling water.

Variations:

for whole wheat pasta, substitute 1/2 cup whole wheat flour for 1/2 cup of the unbleached flour

for tomato pasta, add 2 tablespoons double concentrated tomato paste

for spinach pasta, add 1/4 cup finely puréed spinach

for herb pasta, add 1 tablespoon together dried basil and oregano, and 1/4 teaspoon garlic powder

SHRIMP AND GARDEN VEGETABLES

Fresh garden vegetables, sun-dried tomatoes, and a perfect amount of garlic and red pepper, make a tasty background for plump pink shrimp.

3 tablespoons olive oil
2 cloves garlic, chopped fine
1/4 teaspoon dried crushed red pepper flakes
1/2 of a green bell pepper, sliced thin
1/2 of a red bell pepper, sliced thin
1/4 lb. green beans, cut the length of the pepper slices
10 to 12 ounce medium or large shrimp,
washed, shelled, and deveined
2 tablespoons sliced oil-packed sun-dried tomatoes, drained
2 tablespoons chopped parsley

Heat the olive oil in a large skillet. Add the garlic and crushed red pepper flakes. Stir. Add the beans and the peppers, and sauté until the vegetables just begin to get tender, about five minutes. Add the shrimp, and cook, stirring constantly, until they turn pink, another 3 to 4 minutes. Add the sun dried tomatoes and parsley and remove from heat. Pour over pasta in a large pasta bowl, toss lightly, and serve immediately.

LEMON SOUFFLE

This is an old-fashioned kind of dessert, light and refreshing.

1 cup sugar
1 tablespoon butter
2 tablespoons flour
Zest and juice of one lemon
2 eggs, separated
1 cup milk
1/2 cup whipping cream, whipped
with 1 tablespoon sugar and 1 teaspoon vanilla
1/2 cup fresh blueberries, raspberries, or strawberries

Preheat oven to 350 degrees. Cream sugar with butter, add flour. Add lemon zest and juice. Combine egg yokes and milk, add to lemon mixture. Beat egg white separately until stiff; fold into lemon mixture. Pour into 4 individual 6-ounce baking dishes. Place baking dishes in a pan of hot water, and bake for 30 minutes, until top is lightly browned. There will be a cake-like layer on top, and a custard layer about half way down. Cool, then chill for at least an hour. To serve, add a generous dollop of whipped cream, and sprinkle with fresh berries.

Refrigerate any remaining souffles; enjoy them the next day.

SERVING SPRING TO YOUR LOVER

Add a tiny bouquet of dandelions, violets, or lily-of-the-valley from your yard to each place setting, and to your hors d'oeuvre plate.

Arrange the brie, cracker bread, and green grapes on a large serving platter. Drink your Martini or German Reisling with it, taking plenty of time to enjoy the combination of flavors.

Move on to your salad, served from the kitchen on salad plates, and your focaccia, warmed, cut into pie shaped pieces, and wrapped in a napkin in a basket. Put some softened butter on the table, on a small plate, with a wooden butter spreader.

It will take a few minutes to cook the pasta and shrimp for your entrée. Clear the table and pour the Chardonnay or white Burgundy in the meantime. Serve the entrée from a very large pasta bowl, using a many-pronged pasta server, or a fork and large spoon.

Whip the cream, make the coffee, and pour the sparkling Demi Sec or Asti Spumanti. Pile on the whipped cream, sprinkle on the berries, and serve the lemon souffle from the dishes in which it was baked, placed on small plates or doilies.

Chapter 12

SUNSHINE AND FLOWERS

Gazpacho

*Green Salad
with Strawberries and Poppy Seed Dressing*

Whole Wheat Rolls

Asparagus Spears and Grilled Salmon Filets

Lemon Rice

*Honeydew Splashed with Lime,
Assorted Dessert Cheeses*

Fino Sherry

*Willamet Valley Pinot Noir
or white Alsatian Wine*

Coffee and German Auslese Wine

*S*erve this refreshing dinner outside if you can, on a deck or patio or in the back yard, or create the illusion of being outside by surrounding yourself with bunches of daisies and peonies. The delicate colors in the food would be enhanced by a white tablecloth and napkins, and blue and white china plates. Use pure white candles, and protect the flame from the breeze with glass chimneys.

INGREDIENTS AND PLANNING

Check each recipe; make a list of the ingredients you don't have on hand. Check your liquor cabinet and wine cellar. Don't forget a stop at the liquor store if necessary.

Buy a fresh salmon filet, weighing about twelve ounces. Try to get a thin filet from the tail end, rather than a thicker one from further up the body. There will be fewer bones, and it will grill or broil more easily.

With any luck, you started your planning a few days ago, so that you now have a ripe honeydew melon waiting on your counter top. It is difficult to find a ripe honeydew in the grocery store, but if you didn't plan quite far enough ahead, ask the green grocer for help.

Most of your meal will come from the produce department tonight. Go down the list of gazpacho ingredients; make sure you don't miss any, including fresh dill. Look for crisp, thin, fresh asparagus, a compact head of romaine with no discoloration on the outer leaves, and small, ripe, bright red strawberries for your salad.

If you don't have time to make the rolls yourself, buy some at a bakery.

Go to a specialty cheese store, and experiment with dessert cheeses. The triple créme cheeses are gloriously rich to the point of being decadent; a Port Salut or Gourmandise is a bit more restrained, but still delicious. See what else you like.

We recommend growing peonies in your yard, or at least living next door to someone who does. Their fragrance is one of the defining characteristics of spring, and they can be hard to find in florist's shops. Daisies, on the other hand, are plentiful everywhere. If you can't get peonies, get lots and lots of daisies.

Try listening to some classical guitar music while you sip your gazpacho; Segovia would be perfect. You could stick with classical, or move on to Earl Klugh's jazz guitar; his Midnight in San Juan album is especially nice.

TO DO AHEAD

Most of this meal goes together just before serving it, with two crucial exceptions: It's always a good idea to get your baking done early in the day. Start the rolls in the morning; they have to rise twice, once in the bowl and once in the pans. Yeast works faster than normal in warm weather, so watch the dough rather than the clock.

Gazpacho must be served very cold; it should chill for at least 4 hours, so put that together early in the day, too.

Arrange your daisies and peonies as soon as you pick them or get them home from the flower shop.

Check you table linens to make sure you have a fresh, white tablecloth and napkins ready to use, and not lost in the laundry room.

You can make your salad dressing ahead of time; refrigerate it until you are ready to use it. Clean the asparagus, and wash the salad greens. If your strawberries are quite ripe, you don't want to slice them or add them to the salad until shortly before you will be serving it.

Take your dessert cheeses out of the refrigerator early enough that you can serve them at room temperature.

TASKS FOR CHILDREN

Your preschooler will be an invaluable assistant when you make the rolls, especially when it comes time to divide the dough into all those little pieces. Have a three to six year old help you keep track by counting them, and making sure only three get into each muffin cup. Preschoolers are also very good at rolling the pieces of dough into little golf balls.

Assign a preschooler to staff the food processor or blender while you make the gazpacho; the on-off switch is pretty interesting at this age. Teach them when to turn it off and leave it off, and teach them not to use the machine in a careless and purposeless way. A preschooler could also have a good time spreading olive oil on the salmon, or stirring poppy seeds into the salad dressing.

Gazpacho provides an excellent opportunity for a six to nine year old to practice the basics of vegetable chopping. Because the vegetables will be puréed in the food processor or blender, the chopping need not be precise, and the pieces need not be nicely shaped, or especially small. While your helper is at it, have him or her measure and combine the rest of the gazpacho ingredients, too, and then move on to preparing the salad greens, slicing the strawberries, and mixing the salad dressing. Teach a child this age how to clean and trim asparagus, how to make rice, and how to arrange a nice looking plate of cheeses.

Six to nine year olds are good table setters. Teach one to practice a bit of artistic flair in doing it, unless you enjoy the task too much to delegate it.

With the possible exception of grilling the salmon, this meal could be prepared in its entirety by your nine to twelve year old, with you in the background to help as needed. The dough for the rolls is easy to mix and knead, the process of shaping them is fun, and the end result is very gratifying.

Likewise, the gazpacho is fun and easy to make, and provides a very interesting way for kids to get their vegetables. The salad dressing also goes together easily, and the poppy seed distribution gives a clear indication of how well the dressing is mixed.

Have the young chef prepare the salmon for grilling and the asparagus for steaming. Cooking the lemon rice will be no problem, and neither will creating an artistic arrangement for your honeydew melon and dessert cheeses.

SHARING THE WORK

At the appropriate time,

COOK A	COOK B:
serves cocktails	serves gazpacho
lights candles	
dresses salad	warms rolls
grills salmon	cooks rice
pours wine	cooks asparagus
makes coffee	clears the table
serves dessert	

GAZPACHO

Beautiful to look at, tasty, and ice cold, gazpacho is a great way to begin a springtime supper.

1 large, ripe tomato, chopped
1/2 green bell pepper, chopped
1/2 red bell pepper, chopped
1/2 cucumber, chopped
1 shallot, chopped
1 leek, white part only, chopped
1 clove garlic, chopped
1/4 cup olive oil
1/2 cup bottled tomato juice
3 tablespoons red wine vinegar
1/4 teaspoon salt
1 tablespoon fresh dill, chopped
Freshly ground black pepper to taste
1/8 teaspoon ground cumin
1/8 teaspoon cayenne pepper
2 carrots, peeled
2 green onions, trimmed

Combine tomato, peppers, cucumber, shallot, leek, and garlic in a blender, or the bowl of a food processor fitted with a steal blade. Process until well blended.

Combine olive oil, tomato juice, vinegar, and salt in small bowl, mix well, and add to mixture in food processor. Process again until well blended. Add dill, pepper, cumin, and cayenne. Process again until well blended.

Transfer mixture to a bowl with a lid which seals tightly. Chill for at least 4 hours.

To serve, spoon into two soup bowls or large soup mugs. Garnish each with a whole carrot and green onions.

GREEN SALAD WITH STRAWBERRIES AND POPPY SEED DRESSING

We sometimes serve this salad around Christmas time, because of the holiday colors. It is also a delight to the eye and the palate in springtime.

1/4 cup mayonnaise
3 tablespoons sugar
1 tablespoon poppy seeds
1 tablespoon milk
1 tablespoon raspberry vinegar
1/2 small head romaine,
washed, leaves torn into pieces
6 center slices of a red onion,
separated into circles
1/2 pint fresh strawberries,
washed and sliced

Combine the mayonnaise, sugar, poppy seeds, milk, and vinegar in a small bowl. Toss the lettuce, onion, and strawberries together in a large salad bowl. Just before serving, pour the dressing over the salad, and toss again.

WHOLE WHEAT ROLLS

These have a clover leaf shape, with three sections that pull apart easily. The dough could just as well be shaped into hot dog or hamburger buns.

1 cup lukewarm (105° - 115° f) milk
1/4 cup honey
1 tablespoon (1 packet) active dry yeast
1 cup whole wheat flour
1 teaspoon salt
1 tablespoon butter, melted and cooled
1 egg, lightly beaten
2 cups unbleached white flour

Pour milk into a large mixing bowl, stir in honey, and sprinkle yeast on top. Set aside in a warm place for about ten minutes to dissolve. Add the whole wheat flour, salt, butter, egg, and 1-1/2 cups of the unbleached flour; mix. Turn the dough out onto a lightly floured board.

Begin kneading, and work in the last 1/2 cup of the unbleached flour. Continue kneading until all the flour is worked in, and the dough is smooth and no longer sticky. Form it into a ball. Lightly oil your bread bowl, and return the dough to it, turning it over once or twice so all of it is lightly oiled. Cover with a dampened dish towel, and set aside in a warm place until doubled in bulk, about 1 hour.

Punch the dough down, turn it out onto the lightly floured board, and knead briefly. Grease 2 six-cup muffin pans. Divide the dough in half, each half in thirds, and each third in half again, so you have twelve pieces of dough. Taking them one at a time, divide each into thirds, and roll each third into a ball about the size of a golf ball. Place all three close together in one muffin cup. Continue until all the cups are full.

If you want to, you can shape some or all of the twelve pieces of dough into hamburger or hot dog buns; place them on a lightly greased 12x15x1-inch baking sheet.

Cover again with the dampened towel, and set aside in a warm place until doubled in bulk, about another hour.

Preheat the oven to 375 degrees. Bake the rolls for 10 to 12 minutes, until they are golden brown on top, and sound hollow when tapped. Cool on a rack.

Store or freeze in a tightly sealed plastic bag.

GRILLED SALMON FILET

Delicate pink salmon and bright green asparagus make lovely companions on a plate.

1 salmon filet (about 12 ounces)
1 tablespoon olive oil
12 fresh asparagus spears,
washed and trimmed
2 lemon wedges

Heat the grill. Rub the olive oil over both sides of the salmon filet, and place it flesh side down on a double sheet of aluminum foil. Turn up the sides of the aluminum foil all around, making a pan. Grill in a closed grill, and turn after about 3 minutes. Continue grilling until the edges begin to get a little brown and crispy, and the salmon looks firm, about 5 minutes all together. The exact amount of time will depend on the thickness of the filet, and on how hot the grill. If your grill does not have a cover, it will take a little longer. To broil: cover a broiling pan with foil, rub the salmon with olive oil, put it skin side down on the foil, broil about 5 minutes. Unless the filet is unusually thick, it is not necessary to turn it.

Asparagus Spears: Meanwhile, cook the asparagus spears until they are crisp-tender; microwave on high for about 2 minutes or steam for about 5 minutes.

LEMON RICE

Use basmati rice, an extra-long grain white rice. Look for it at a wholefoods coop or a specialty gourmet store.

2 tablespoons olive oil
2 green onions, including green part, chopped
1 clove garlic, chopped
1 cup chicken broth
1 cup water
1 cup uncooked long grain white rice
2 teaspoons lemon zest
1/2 teaspoon salt
1/4 teaspoon dry mustard
3 drops red pepper sauce

Heat olive oil in a small sauce pan. Add scallions and garlic, cook until tender, about three minutes. Add the rest of the ingredients, stir. Reduce the heat, cover the pan, and cook until all the liquid is absorbed, about 10 minutes.

HONEYDEW SPLASHED WITH LIME, ASSORTED DESSERT CHEESES

Most honeydew melons that you find in the supermarket are several days from ripeness, so you need to shop for it ahead of time. The skin of an unripe honeydew is smooth and almost velvety to the touch. As it ripens, the skin takes on a waxy, or slightly tacky feel, which starts at one end, and spreads over the whole melon. The ends become slightly soft when pushed with your thumb, but not as soft as a ripe cantaloupe feels. You can keep a ripe honeydew for three or four days in the refrigerator.

For dessert cheeses, try Port Salut, Gourmandise with Kirsh, or triple créme cheeses such as Saint Andre or Brillat-savarin.

1/2 of a ripe honeydew melon, chilled, and cut in two
1/2 of lime, cut in four wedges
About 1/4 pound all together of dessert cheeses,
at room temperature

Serve each 1/4 melon on a plate with two lime wedges. Splash the lime on the melon as you eat your way through it. Serve the cheeses on a separate plate.

SERVING YOUR SPRINGTIME SUPPER

Take one or two daisies from the bouquet, and insert them in the folds of your white napkins.

Serve your gazpacho from the kitchen, in china soup bowls, or large pottery soup mugs, garnished with carrot sticks and scallions. Drink your Fino Sherry from heavy stemmed glasses.

The salad looks lovely in a big glass salad bowl; bring it to the table, and serve it onto glass salad plates. Line a bread basket with a white napkin, warm the roles in it, and serve them with the salad.

Pour your dinner wine (Pinot Noir from the Willamet Valley, or white Alsatian). Serve the entrée from the kitchen, arranging the salmon filet, asparagus spears, and lemon rice on your blue and white china dinner plates. Garnish with a lemon wedge.

Keep the melon chilled until you are ready to serve it, on dessert plates, topped with a lime wedge. Arrange your assortment of cheeses on a serving plate. Pour your coffee into china cups, and your Auslese into stemmed wine glasses.

Chapter 13

SAVORY SUMMER

*Skewered Cherry Tomatoes and Cucumbers
with Avocado Slices*

Blueberry Muffins

*Pasta Salad
with Marinated Chicken Breasts*

Julienned Carrots and Summer Squash

Fruit Tart with Chocolate Pecan Crust

*Long Island Iced Tea (see recipe, page 63)
or Vinho Verde*

*Light Zinfandel
or Australian Chardonnay*

*Coffee and Chambord
or Vin de Glacier*

*T*he addition of warm, sweet blueberry muffins to this cool array of summer vegetables makes for an interesting contrast in this savory meal. If you have some brightly colored pottery plates, they would provide an excellent background, especially on brightly colored plaid place mats. Use napkins to match, and stuff them into cobalt blue wine glasses. Get a few bunches of gladiolus in different colors, and stand them up in tall vases on the floor around your table. Add an array of candles to complete the setting.

INGREDIENTS AND PLANNING

Check each recipe; make a list of the ingredients you don't have on hand. Check your liquor cabinet and wine cellar. Don't forget to stop at the liquor store if necessary.

The best way to shop for this meal is an early morning trip to the farmer's market. If that is not possible, do the best you can in the produce department of your favorite grocery store.

You'll need cherry tomatoes, a nice cucumber, and a ripe avocado. You'll need bell peppers in red, green, and yellow, and you could try orange and purple if you like. You'll need scallions, carrots, a summer squash, fresh parsley, and fresh basil.

You'll need a pint of blueberries; what you don't use in the muffins can go into the fruit tarts. Look at the raspberries, strawberries, peaches, plums, nectarines, and grapes; choose the best, most beautiful, tastiest, and most perfect for your fruit tarts.

Buy your gladiolus while you're there.

Dried pasta works fine in the salad, but if you have a source for fresh bow tie pasta, by all means make use of it. Actually, any pasta shape will do, including linguini, which is relatively easy to find fresh.

You could make your own bow ties. Use the plain pasta recipe in Chapter Twelve. Roll the dough with your pasta machine, and cut it into 1-1/2x2-inch rectangles with a fluted pastry cutter; squeeze the rectangles together firmly in the center to make the bow tie shape. If you decide to do this, give yourself plenty of time, then leave the bow ties in a single layer on a sheet of wax paper to dry slightly before cooking them. Remember that they will cook very quickly.

Buy your chicken breasts fresh, unless you had some stored in your freezer. If so, thaw them overnight in the refrigerator. In any case, make sure they are completely thawed, rinse and dry them thoroughly, and remove the skins before placing them in the marinade.

When you select your music, think about some cool jazz on a hot summer night. Miles Davis, John Coltraine, Dizzy Gillespie, Thelonious Monk, Billie Holiday, Louis Armstrong, Woody Herman, Benny Goodman, Chuck Mangione; add to the list as you like.

TO DO AHEAD

Most of this meal is done ahead, since it needs to chill for several hours.

Following the general rule of getting your baking done early on hot summer days, start with your fruit tart shells and blueberry muffins. The tarts should be chilled, but the muffins should be served warm. If you like, you can deviate from the rule, and make the muffins just before serving, so you won't need to reheat them.

After baking the shells, let them cool, then fill them with the fruit and glaze, and put them in the refrigerator to chill.

Arrange your gladiolus in tall vases as soon as you get them home.

Prepare the marinade, and begin marinating the chicken breasts in the refrigerator. Make the pasta salad; cover, and chill.

Check your table linen drawer; make sure the place mats and napkins you want for tonight are pressed and ready to use.

Cut the carrot and summer squash into julienne strips, and refrigerate, wrapped or covered tightly until time to cook them.

You can prepare the skewered cherry tomato and cucumber hors d'oeuvre up to an hour ahead; cover and refrigerate if it will be more than about fifteen minutes until you eat it.

TASKS FOR CHILDREN

Find a preschooler who likes getting his or her hands into things, and assign the task of lining the tart tins with the chocolate pecan crust. You can assist by dividing the dough equally, making sure it is spread relatively evenly, and checking for excessive dough snitching. Depending on what fruits you are using, a preschooler could be asked to arrange them artistically in the shells.

Other preschooler tasks include measuring and mixing the dry ingredients for the muffins, pouring in the liquid ingredients, sorting the blueberries, and adding them to the batter. A preschooler could also make sure the pasta salad is adequately stirred, both before and after the dressing is added.

A six to nine year old could be pretty much responsible for the fruit tart shells, with help as needed to melt the butter or take the shells out of the oven. One could make the muffins, after careful training in how to mix in blueberries without breaking them.

Shredding scallions into lengthwise strips and cutting matchstick sized pieces of carrot and summer squash are tasks for more advanced chefs, but a six to nine year old would do fine cutting thin slices of peppers or thick slices of cucumber. One could easily mix the marinade for the chicken, the dressing for the pasta salad, and the mustard sauce for the hors d'oeuvre, not to mention skewering the cherry tomatoes and cucumbers and carefully peeling an avocado.

Assign a six to nine year old to set the table, unless it is a task you enjoy.

If you are lucky enough to have a child in the nine to twelve year old range who has spent a little time in the kitchen, leave your menu out on the kitchen table and spend the day sitting in the porch swing reading a murder mystery; all of your advance preparation could be done by the time you get to the end.

Alternatively, you could ask your child to be in charge of making the blueberry muffins in a timely manner, so that they can be served fresh from the oven when you finish your hors d'oeuvre. He or she could sauté your julienned vegetables at the same time, leaving you and your sweetheart free to enjoy your cocktails outside, savoring the smell of the chicken as it cooks on the grill.

SHARING THE WORK

At the appropriate time,

COOK A	COOK B:
serves the hors d'oeuvre	serves cocktails or wine
lights candles	grills chicken
warms muffins	
sautés vegetables	serves pasta salad
pours wine	
clears the table	makes coffee
	serves dessert

SKEWERED CHERRY TOMATOES AND CUCUMBERS WITH AVOCADO SLICES

A tangy mustard sauce is a pretty background, and adds a delightful flavor with these vegetables.

1 tablespoon honey mustard
1 tablespoon walnut oil
1 tablespoon chopped fresh basil leaves
8 cherry tomatoes, washed and stemmed
4 cucumber slices, about 1/2-inch thick, halved
1 ripe avocado, sliced into eighths

Combine the mustard, oil, and basil in a small bowl. When it is well mixed, spread it over the bottom of a small serving platter or dinner plate. Put one cherry tomato and one halved cucumber slice on each of eight toothpicks, so that a little of the toothpick sticks out at each end. Arrange them on the plate over the mustard sauce. Arrange the avocado slices around the edges. Serve at once.

BLUEBERRY MUFFINS

Not just for breakfast by any means, blueberry muffins make a fine addition to a summer supper.

2-1/2 cups flour
1/3 cup sugar
1/2 teaspoon salt
1 tablespoon baking powder
1 tablespoon grated lemon zest
2 eggs, lightly beaten
1-1/4 cups milk
1/4 cup butter, melted
1-1/2 cups blueberries, washed and sorted

Preheat the oven to 400 degrees. Lightly grease two 6-cup muffin tins. Combine the flour, sugar, salt, baking powder, and lemon zest in a mixing bowl.

Combine the egg, milk, and butter in a separate small bowl.

Pour the egg mixture into the dry ingredients, and stir with a wooden spoon until just combined. Carefully fold in the blueberries in the last few strokes. Spoon the batter into the muffin tins.

Bake for 20 minutes, until the tops of the muffins are lightly browned. Cool for a few minutes before removing them from the pans. Serve warm.

If you make them ahead, cool completely on a rack before storing in a tightly sealed plastic bag. Reheat briefly (less than a minute) in the microwave, or for about five minutes in a 300 degree oven.

PASTA SALAD

For a variation on this salad, slice a cooked chicken breast into thin strips, and toss it with the pasta and vegetables before adding the dressing.

10 ounces bow-tie pasta, cooked, drained, and cooled
4 green onions, green part included,
thinly sliced lengthwise into 2-inch strips
1/2 green bell pepper, sliced thin
1/2 red bell pepper, sliced thin
1/2 yellow bell pepper, sliced thin
1/4 cup mayonnaise
2 tablespoons olive oil
1 tablespoon red wine vinegar
1/4 teaspoon salt
freshly ground black pepper to taste

Combine the pasta and the vegetables in a large pasta bowl. Combine the mayonnaise, olive oil, vinegar, salt, and pepper in a small bowl, stir with a fork until smooth and very well blended. Pour it over the salad, and stir well with a large spoon, until the salad and dressing are combined. Cover with tin foil or plastic wrap, and chill for several hours before serving.

MARINATED CHICKEN BREASTS

This also makes a great marinade for steak. Try marinating a tougher cut, such as a round steak or flank steak, for several hours, then grilling it. You'll be amazed at how tender and tasty it is.

1/4 cup olive oil
1/4 cup dry sherry
2 tablespoons balsamic vinegar
2 cloves garlic, crushed
1 tablespoon honey
1/2 teaspoon dry mustard
Freshly ground black pepper to taste
2 chicken breast halves,
washed, dried, skin removed

Combine all the ingredients except the chicken breasts in a medium sized bowl. Mix well. Add the chicken breasts, and turn them over a few times, so they are well coated with the marinade. Cover the bowl, and refrigerate for at least four hours, turning the chicken occasionally. Heat the grill or broiler. Cook the chicken breasts for approximately 30 minutes, until they are well browned on the outside, and done throughout. Turn them occasionally during cooking, and brush with the marinade.

JULIENNED CARROTS AND SUMMER SQUASH

Arranged in a little mound on your plate, they look like the summer sunshine.

1 small carrot, peeled
1 small, yellow, summer squash, washed
1 tablespoon olive oil
2 tablespoons chopped fresh parsley
Salt and freshly ground black pepper to taste

Cut the carrot and summer squash into matchstick sized pieces, about 2 inches long, and of uniform width. Heat the olive oil over medium heat in a small frying pan. Add the vegetables, parsley, salt and pepper. Lightly sauté until crisp-tender, about 5 minutes. Serve immediately.

FRUIT TARTS WITH CHOCOLATE PECAN CRUST

You'll have to share these with your children. Try to save out a couple, though, because they taste even better the next day.

1/4 cup butter
1/4 cup unsweetened cocoa powder
1/4 cup powdered sugar
1/4 cup flour
1/2 cup ground pecans
1 egg, lightly beaten
1/2 teaspoon vanilla
1/4 cup apple jelly
2 tablespoons Grand Marnier or Chambord
1 teaspoon grated lemon zest
1-1/2 half cups fresh fruit or berries,
cleaned, sorted, and pealed if necessary
(Use any combination of raspberries, blueberries, or strawberries, peach, nectarine, or plum slices, or seedless red or green grape halves.)
1/2 cup whipping cream,whipped with
1 tablespoon sugar and 1 teaspoon vanilla (optional)

Preheat oven to 350 degrees. Lightly grease 8 four-inch tart tins, a nine-inch tart pan with a removable bottom, or, if none of these are available, a nine-inch pie pan.

Ground pecans are sometimes available in the nut department of grocery stores. Otherwise, grind them yourself in a blender or food processor, or chop them as fine as you can with a nut chopper.

Melt the butter and cocoa powder together over low heat in a small sauce pan. Remove from heat, and add sugar, flour, ground pecans, egg, and vanilla. Combine well. Press the mixture into the bottom of the prepared tins or pan. Bake for 10 minutes. Cool in the pans.

Melt the apple jelly over low heat with the liqueur and lemon zest. Place the berries or fruit in a bowl, and pour on the glaze. Stir very gently, so that all the fruit is coated, but none is broken or crushed. Arrange the glazed fruit in the tart shell or shells. (If your fruit or berries are very delicate, like ripe raspberries, arrange it in the tart shells first, and spoon the glaze over it).

Cover, and chill for several hours before serving. To serve, remove the tarts from the tins, or, if you are using a pie pan, cut it as you would a pie. You can garnish with a dab of whipped cream, if you like.

SERVING YOUR SUMMER SUPPER

Tuck a single gladiolus bloom into the napkins stuffed in the wine glasses.

Spread the mustard sauce for your hors d'oeuvre over the bottom of a large serving plate. Arrange the skewered vegetables and avocado slices on it in a single layer. Set a small salad plate at each place. Drink your Vinho Verde, or Long Island Iced Tea cocktail with your hors d'oeuvre. If you choose the cocktail, drink it slowly, and keep adding ice to your glass; it could last you through dinner.

Line a basket with one of your brightly colored napkins, and warm the blueberry muffins in it. Put a small dish of softened butter on the table, along with a wooden butter spreader. Serve the pasta salad from a large pasta bowl on the table. Serve the chicken and vegetables from the kitchen, leaving room on the plates for pasta salad.

When you are ready for dessert, remove the fruit tarts from the tart pans (or, if you made one big tart, cut into pie shaped pieces). Arrange them on a large serving plate. Put a dessert plate, decorated with a doily, at each place. Pour your liqueur (Chambord or Vin de Glacier) into cordial glasses, and your coffee into brightly colored cups or mugs.

Chapter 14

SUMMER LOVE

Mussels Steamed in White Wine
or Shrimp Cocktail

Garden-grown Tomato and Fresh Basil Salad

Rosemary Bread Sticks

Grilled Steak Served with New Potatoes

Strawberry Short Cake

Gin and Tonic (see recipe, page 63)
or Muscadet White Wine

California Zinfandel
or Beer

Coffee and Brandy

*H*ere's a perfectly simple, straight-forward, old-fashioned, summer dinner. Fill a big pottery jug with zinnias and snapdragons, set it on your picnic table, and get out those old earthenware plates from your grandmother's summer cabin. Use woven place mats, and homespun napkins. Consider having a beer with dinner, or drink your wine from unadorned tumblers instead of stemmed glasses. Surround yourselves with lots of citronella candles; they are effective bug repellents if you use enough. Since mussels are sometimes hard to find, we offer a choice of hors d'oeuvres; either one is a great beginning.

INGREDIENTS AND PLANNING

Check each recipe; make a list of the ingredients you don't have on hand. Check your liquor cabinet and wine cellar, and your refrigerator for beer. Don't forget a stop at the liquor store if necessary.

Go to your fish market for fresh mussels. Buy as many as you think you will want for your hors d'oeuvre; six to nine each is usually enough. Ask the fish seller to choose the mussels with tightly closed shells. Some sellers will throw in a few extra in case you end up with some slightly opened shells.

If your hors d'oeuvre will be shrimp cocktail instead of steamed mussels, it requires the biggest, freshest shrimp you can find. Usually six is enough for each of you. Check to make sure you have an interesting shrimp sauce.

The next stop is the farmer's market for your tomatoes. In addition to being large, very red, and just a bit soft when squeezed, they must have been ripened on the vine, by the sun, in the open air. Anything else is merely second rate. You can stop short of asking for a certificate of guarantee about the conditions under which they were grown, but your tomato experience will be significantly enhanced by learning to recognize those grown in a real garden. The ultimate test, next to the taste test, of course, is trying to peel one. Tomatoes grown in a real garden outdoors and allowed to ripen on the vine shed their peelings as easily as you shed your swim suit after a day at the beach.

While you're at the farmer's market, pick up bunches of fresh basil and fresh parsley, a pound or two of very small, round, new potatoes, and a pint of strawberries. We could go on and on about the difference between garden-grown and commercial strawberries, too, but as long as you choose some that are very red and fully ripe, you'll probably be okay.

If zinnias and snapdragons don't grow in your yard, the farmer's market is probably the best place to find them.

When you buy your steak, buy a smaller amount of a very good cut, such as New York strip, Filet Mignon, or Chateaubriand, rather than a large amount of, say, round steak. Many butchers make very lean beef available; make sure it is also very well trimmed. For maximum tenderness, steak must be at least completely thawed, and some say it should reach room temperature, before it is ever brought near the grill or broiler, which must be very hot.

Let some of the old country and western greats entertain you tonight. Try Hank Williams (Senior, not Junior), Patsy Cline, or Les Paul and Mary Ford. For more of a folk feeling, try the Weavers, the Kingston Trio, Robin and Linda Williams, or pre-1970 Gordon Lightfoot. If none of those are appealing, try an album of hammered dulcimer or harp music, or maybe an all Chopin evening.

To Do Ahead

Start by making the bread sticks. They are the only component of this meal that will take any time at all to prepare, though most of the time you can pretty much leave the dough alone to do what it needs to do. When they are baked and have cooled completely, store them in a tightly sealed plastic bag until supper time. If time is short, add bread sticks to your grocery list instead of planning to make them.

While the oven is hot, make the short cakes, and store them in a tightly sealed plastic bag once they have cooled, too. On the other hand, they are very easy and quick to make, and you might decide to do it just before dinner, so they will still be a little warm when you are ready for dessert.

Shrimp cocktail needs to chill for several hours, so if that will be your hors d'oeuvre, make it fairly early in the day. If you will be steaming mussels instead, you can scrub all the seaweed and sand off the shells, and keep them in the refrigerator until you are ready to cook them.

Arrange your flowers as soon as you pick them or get them home.

Check to make sure your place mats and napkins are ready to use.

You can make your tomato salad an hour or so before you will want to eat it; keep it in the refrigerator along with the strawberries, which you can clean at about the same time. If you like, sprinkle the berries with a little sugar, and they will manufacture a light syrup as they wait.

TASKS FOR CHILDREN

Making bread sticks provides preschoolers several opportunities to exercise their skills in sprinkling, pouring, stirring, kneading, and rolling. Have one pour the water into the bowl, sprinkle the yeast on top, and let you know about each resulting change as the yeast dissolves and begins to bubble and froth. Let them help you add the rest of the ingredients, stir and knead the dough, and, when the time comes, shape it into thin pencil-like shapes.

Short cake is another good opportunity for a preschool cooking lesson. Let them measure and stir, and let them plop the dough onto the baking sheet. Since perfect symmetry is the antithesis of the spirit of these particular short cakes, let your preschooler experiment a little when shaping them into cloud-like mounds. Don't handle the dough too much, though, or the cakes won't be tender.

A preschooler could also be handed a small brush and asked to scrub a few mussels. Preschoolers are fascinated by the idea that a little animal lived inside the shell.

Give a six to nine year old a bit more responsibility with each of these tasks, as well as the job of cleaning strawberries, scrubbing and halving new potatoes, chopping parsley, mixing the dressing for the salad, peeling and slicing tomatoes, and arranging them artistically on a plate with the basil. Unless you find setting the table an outlet for your own creative energy, let a six to nine year old do it.

Those in the nine to twelve year old group could go ahead and cook the shrimp for shrimp cocktail, or, after chopping shallots and leeks and measuring half a cup of wine, steam the mussels. They could make either the bread sticks or the short cakes, or both, virtually unassisted. They could cook your potatoes for you while you enjoy your cocktail and hors d'oeuvre on the deck.

One who has been trained to do so, and given the proper long-handled equipment and barbecue mitts, could grill your steak for you. Think about this one, though; if you will be having supper outdoors, you probably want your child indoors. Ask her or him to whip the cream for your dessert, instead.

SHARING THE WORK

At the appropriate time,

COOK A	COOK B:
steams mussels	
or serves shrimp cocktail	serves cocktails or wine
serves tomato salad	
grills steak	cooks potatoes
pours wine	lights citronella candles
makes coffee	clears table
whips cream	serves dessert
pours brandy	

MUSSELS STEAMED IN WHITE WINE

Fresh mussels make an impressive, delicious, and easy hors d'oeuvre.

4 tablespoons butter
1 small shallot, chopped
1 leek, white part only, chopped
12 to 18 fresh mussels, cleaned
Salt and freshly ground black pepper to taste
1/2 cup Muscadet, or other dry white wine
1 clove garlic, chopped fine
1 teaspoon snipped fresh parsley
Lemon slices

Melt 1 tablespoon butter in a deep sauce pan or kettle large enough to hold the mussels. Add the shallot and leek, and sauté gently for two minutes. Add mussels. Sprinkle with salt and freshly ground pepper. Pour in the wine. Cover and steam gently until all the mussels are open, about five minutes. Meanwhile, melt the remaining 3 tablespoons butter over low heat in a small pan. Add the garlic, heat for two minutes. Remove from heat, add the parsley, and stir. Pour into a small dish for dipping. Remove the mussels from the kettle with a slotted spoon, arrange on plates, and garnish with lemon slices.

SHRIMP COCKTAIL

If you can't find fresh mussels, or if you prefer shrimp, try this classic. Experiment with purchased cocktail sauces; some are sweeter, some tangier, and some are tastier.

1 quart water
1 clove garlic
1 stalk celery, chopped, with leaves
1 teaspoon salt
12 very fresh jumbo shrimp,
 shelled and deveined
2 leaves leaf lettuce
2 lemon wedges
cocktail sauce

Combine the water, garlic, celery, and salt in a large sauce pan, bring to a boil, boil rapidly for five minutes. Add shrimp, reduce heat, simmer for three minutes. Drain immediately, and chill for at least two hours. To serve, arrange the shrimp on a bed of leaf lettuce, with a lemon wedge. Dip in your favorite purchased cocktail sauce.

GARDEN-GROWN TOMATO AND FRESH BASIL SALAD

If garden-grown, sun-ripened tomatoes are unavailable from a farmer's market, road side stand, or your own garden, choose another salad. Add some basil to a green salad, for instance, or slice up some cucumbers and scallions and splash them with white wine vinegar.

1 tablespoon extra virgin olive oil
1 teaspoon red wine vinegar
1/4 teaspoon salt
1/4 teaspoon dry mustard
1 large sun-ripened tomato,
 peeled and sliced
1/2 cup loosely packed fresh basil leaves, stems removed

Combine olive oil, red wine vinegar, salt, and dry mustard in a small bowl, mix well with a fork. Arrange tomato slices on a serving plate, decorate with the basil leaves, and drizzle the dressing over it. Serve immediately.

Rosemary Bread Sticks

We like to use kosher salt for these bread sticks because of its coarse texture. You could substitute the same amount of table salt; it would slightly affect the appearance, but not the flavor.

1 cup warm (105° - 115°f) water
1 tablespoon or 1 packet active dry yeast
2 tablespoons olive oil
1 tablespoon diced rosemary, crumbled
2 teaspoons coarse kosher salt
2 1/2 - 3 cups unbleached flour
Coarse kosher salt for sprinkling

Pour the water into a large mixing bowl, sprinkle the yeast on top, and set aside for ten minutes to dissolve.

Stir in the olive oil, rosemary, and salt. Add 2 cups of the flour, mixing well with a wooden spoon. Turn the dough out onto a lightly floured board, and knead well, working in about another half cup of flour, until the dough is smooth and not sticky. Form it into a ball.

Lightly oil your bread bowl, and return the dough to it, turning the ball of dough once or twice so all of it is thinly coated with oil. Cover the bowl with a dampened dish towel, and chill for two hours. (You can chill it overnight, if that is more convenient).

Lightly oil two 12x15x1-inch baking pans. Take the chilled dough out of the bowl, and knead it briefly on the lightly floured board. Break off a piece about the size of a large cherry or a small walnut. Using the remaining flour to prevent sticking, if necessary, roll it on the bread board until it is long and thin — a shape more like a pencil than like a cigar.

Place it on the baking pan. Continue until all the dough is used up, placing the bread sticks about an inch apart on the baking pans. There will be about 30 to 35 bread sticks, depending on how closely they resemble pencils.

Preheat the oven to 400 degrees. Cover the baking pans with a dampened dish towel, and set aside for about half an hour, until the bread sticks begin to look a little bit like cigars. Brush them with a little olive oil, and, if you like, sprinkle them with a little coarse kosher salt.

Bake until they are golden brown, about 15 minutes. Switch the pans on the oven shelves half way through. Cool the bread sticks thoroughly on a rack. They can be stored in a tightly sealed plastic bag.

GRILLED STEAK SERVED WITH NEW POTATOES

Surely, you couldn't let the summer pass without at least one dinner of grilled steak and potatoes.

6 to 8 small new potatoes,
scrubbed and cut in half
1 teaspoon salt
1 tablespoon butter
1 tablespoon snipped parsley
2 New York strip steaks,
each about 6 ounces in weight,and about 1-inch thick

It is not necessary to peal new potatoes. Put them in a large sauce pan with water to cover, and the salt. Bring to a boil, then reduce the heat and simmer for twenty to thirty minutes, until they are fork tender but not beginning to crumble. Drain. Add butter and parsley to the pan, and stir. Set aside.

Take the steaks out of the refrigerator one-half hour before cooking. Heat the grill or broiler. Cook the steaks for about three minutes on each side, but watch them closely. They should be seared to a dark brown on the outside, but remain pink and tender inside. Don't over cook them. To serve, place each steak on a dinner plate with the potatoes.

STRAWBERRY SHORT CAKE

This is the way they did it back home. These short cakes look like cumulus clouds, and taste like heaven. Add some blueberries for a patriotic touch.

1 cup flour
1 tablespoon sugar
1-1/2 teaspoon baking powder
1/2 teaspoon salt

1/2 teaspoon grated lemon zest
3 tablespoons butter or margarine
1/2 cup milk
1 pint fresh strawberries, cleaned
1/2 cup whipping cream,
whipped with 1 tablespoon sugar and 1 teaspoon vanilla

Preheat oven to 425 degrees. Sift together flour, sugar, baking powder, and salt. Add lemon zest. Cut in butter or margarine with a pastry blender. Add milk. Mix with a fork until just combined. Drop 4 equal portions onto a greased baking sheet. Bake for 10 to 12 minutes, until golden brown. Cool on a rack. To serve, cut each short cake in halfcross wise, like you would a hamburger bun. Spoon strawberries and whipped cream onto the bottom half, replace the top half, and spoon on some more. Store leftover short cakes in a tightly sealed plastic bag.

SERVING YOUR SUMMER LOVE

Set a hand fan next to each place, in case the evening is warm.

If your hors d'oeuvre is mussels, arrange them on large dinner plates garnished with lemon, and provide little seafood forks. Pour the dipping butter into a small pottery dish, and set it between you on the table. Include a large basket or pottery bowl in which to put the shells. If you are having the shrimp, you can arrange them in small bowls, on a bed of lettuce, with a lemon wedge, then set the small bowls in larger bowls of crushed ice. Pour the cocktail sauce onto a small plate, and put it between you. In any case, enjoy your Gin and Tonic or Muscadet with your hors d'oeuvre.

Arrange the bread sticks in a basket. Arrange the tomatoes and basil on a pottery serving plate. Serve them both with the steak and new potatoes, on large dinner plates. Pour your beer into tall Pilsner glasses, or pour your Zinfandel into plain tumblers.

Strawberry short cake would look lovely on deep blue dessert plates. Put a small, matching bowl filled with extra whipped cream on the table. Pour your coffee into mugs, and your brandy into large snifters; the brandy should no more than cover the bottom of the snifter, leaving plenty of room to swirl it around and enjoy the bouquet.

Chapter  *15*

ROMANTIC HARVEST

Scallops Steamed with Leeks

Carrot Soup

Tiny Zucchini Muffins

Sweet Orange Chicken
Served with Rice Pilaf and Green Beans

Baked Apples

Bourbon with Club Soda (see recipe, page 62)
or Italian Pinot Grigio

Spätlese Reisling

Coffee and Late Harvest Auslese

*T*here is a chill in the air; evening comes early. Fill your house with the wonderful smells this meal will create. Bring in the last of the chrysanthemums from your garden, and a bunch of bittersweet to arrange in a big blue and white china pitcher. Set your table on a cloth of bright fall colors, with matching napkins. Use wrought iron or pewter candle holders, and a collection of candles to complement your fall color scheme.

Ingredients and Planning

Check each recipe; make a list of the ingredients you don't have on hand. Check your liquor cabinet and wine cellar. Don't forget a stop at the liquor store if necessary.

Purchase 8 ounces fresh scallops; if you will be using frozen scallops, thaw them for several hours in the refrigerator.

Buy your chicken fresh, too. If you will be using frozen chicken, thaw it overnight in the refrigerator, and make sure it is completely thawed before cooking it.

Buy the nicest looking green beans you can find. They should be fairly small, straight, unblemished, and of uniform size. It is not essential that any of the other vegetables — leeks, carrots, zucchini, mushrooms, scallions, and parsley — be fresh that day, but while you're in the produce department, you might as well pick them up, too.

Likewise, the apples need not be fresh that day. Apple orchards exist in many parts of the country, and many welcome visitors. Some even give you a chance to pick your own. A trip to your local orchard with your children on a crisp autumn day makes a fun family excursion, and you can supply yourself with plenty of apples for baking and eating, not to mention jellies, preserves, honey, and, if you're lucky, a few varieties of honey mustard.

If you have no chrysanthemums in your garden, stop at a florist to buy some. They come in a wide variety of colors, so you can get enough to complement both the color scheme in your house, and the fall colors outside. If you buy bittersweet, it need not be put in water, and will still last long enough to decorate your house until Christmas time.

Think of some cozy, intimate dinner music, for your Romantic Harvest — Keith Jarret's *Köln Concert,* perhaps, or Rachmaninoff's *Vocalise,* Bach's *Brandenburg Concertos,* or Jean-Pierre Rampal's and Claude Bolling's *Suite for Flute and Jazz Piano.*

To Do Ahead

The zucchini muffins are the fussiest part of this menu; get them out of the way early in the day. You can reheat them in the microwave or in a 300 degree oven at supper time.

Make the carrot soup early, too, so it has time to stand around perfecting its flavors.

You can get the chicken ready to bake early, if you want to; refrigerate it in the baking dish until about half an hour before you want to put it in the oven. Prepare the baked apples, and refrigerate them, too. Dipping the cut tops in lemon juice will prevent discoloring. Since the chicken and the apples bake at the same temperature for roughly the same amount of time, you can bake them together when the time comes.

Arrange the flowers or bittersweet branches as soon as you bring them in.

If you haven't used your autumn tablecloth and napkins since last autumn, check your linen drawer to be sure they are in a ready condition, and not a wrinkled condition; plan time to iron them if necessary.

When the chicken is about half done, start the rice, and start reheating your soup. By the time you finish steaming and enjoying the scallops, your soup will be ready.

By the time you finish the soup, the entrée will be ready, although you'll need a few minutes to cook the beans.

By the time you finish your entrée, the baked apples will be perfect, if you have left them in the warm (but turned off) oven.

TASKS FOR CHILDREN

Set a preschooler to the task of combining the dry ingredients for the zucchini muffins, and then pouring in the liquid ingredients. A supervised preschooler could spoon the batter into the muffin tins. If you use a food processor to grate the zucchini, and to purée the carrots for soup, let your preschooler turn it on and off, taking the opportunity to offer instruction in its appropriate use.

Your six to nine year old helpers could also add the seasonings to the soup, and mix the orange sauce for the chicken, and the stuffing for the baked apples. Chopping nuts is an especially gratifying task for them. Have one chop the vegetables for the rice pilaf, and prepare the green beans. Have one set the table, too, unless you like to do it yourself.

There is nothing in this menu that is beyond the skill of a nine to twelve year old who has had a little training. If you don't mind having one hanging around in the kitchen during your romantic rendezvous, you could use it as an excellent lesson in coordinating the timing for various parts of a meal. Otherwise, just ask for some help with the do-ahead parts. Ask one to make the muffins, make the soup, make the orange sauce, or stuff the apples for baking.

Sharing the Work

At the appropriate time,

Cook A	Cook B:
starts cooking rice	steams scallops
makes cocktails	
serves soup	warms muffins
cooks beans	pours wine
serves entrée	
clears table	makes coffee
	serves dessert

Scallops Steamed with Leeks

Bay scallops are the smaller ones; you can steam them whole. Sea scallops are much larger, and will steam more evenly if you slice them in half or thirds first. Either way, this is an elegant and delicious hors d'oeuvre.

2 tablespoons butter
1 clove garlic, chopped
1 leek, white part only, sliced
2 tablespoons bottled clam juice
2 tablespoons lemon juice
8 ounces fresh bay scallops or sea scallops
1 tablespoon fresh parsley, chopped
2 lemon wedges

Melt the butter over low heat, add the garlic and leek, and sauté gently until tender, about 3 minutes. Add the clam juice and lemon juice; bring to a boil.

Transfer the mixture to a shallow glass baking dish; choose a dish that will fit inside a covered frying pan or kettle for steaming. Arrange the scallops in a single layer over the leek mixture.

Pour about 1 inch of water into a large frying pan or kettle, place the baking dish in it, and cover tightly with the pan or kettle cover, or with a sheet of aluminum foil. Steam over medium-high heat until the scallops turn opaque, 8 to 10 minutes.

To serve, remove the scallops, and just a few pieces of leek, with a slotted spoon, and arrange them on two serving plates. Sprinkle with the parsley, and garnish each plate with a lemon wedge.

CARROT SOUP

This is a great way to get your vegetables. You can add a bit more of the cayenne pepper if you like things extra spicy.

2 tablespoons butter
1 medium yellow onion, chopped
1 stalk celery with leaves, chopped
4 medium carrots, chopped
1 (14-1/2 ounce) can low-salt chicken broth
1 teaspoon sugar
1/2 teaspoon freshly grated nutmeg
1/4 teaspoon dried thyme leaves
1/8 teaspoon cayenne pepper
salt to taste
up to 1/2 cup water, if needed
2 small sprigs fresh parsley

Melt the butter in frying pan over medium-low heat. Add onion and celery, and sauté until tender but not brown, about 5 minutes. Add carrots, and 1/2 cup of the chicken broth. Cover, and simmer until the carrots are tender, about 20 minutes. Add a little more of the chicken broth as needed if the liquid simmers away.

Transfer the mixture to the bowl of a food processor fitted with the steal blade. Add the sugar, nutmeg, thyme, cayenne pepper, and salt. Purée until smooth. If you don't have a food processor, purée it in a blender, or by putting it through a food mill.

Transfer the purée to a sauce pan, and stir in the remaining chicken broth. If the soup is thicker than you like it to be, add the water slowly to thin it. Bring to a boil, and remove from heat.

You can serve the soup at this point, but letting it stand for a few hours enhances the flavor. Cool it, then refrigerate until time to eat. Reheat it over low heat until it just reaches a boil. Spoon into soup bowls, and garnish each with a sprig of parsley.

TINY ZUCCHINI MUFFINS

Making the muffins tiny means that you can pop them whole into your mouth, where, as the saying goes, they melt. The muffin tins we use for this recipe have twelve cups, each 3/4-inch deep and 1-3/4-inches across. We found them in the cookware section of our favorite grocery store. If you can't find any, use the regular size; the muffins will be just as good, though they will need about 20 minutes to bake.

1 cup flour
1/2 cup sugar
1/2 cup walnuts, chopped
1 teaspoon grated lemon zest
1/2 teaspoon salt
1/2 teaspoon baking soda
1/4 teaspoon baking powder
1 teaspoon cinnamon
1/2 teaspoon ground allspice
1/8 teaspoon ground cloves
2 eggs, lightly beaten
1/3 cup vegetable oil
1 teaspoon vanilla
1 cup unpealed zucchini, grated

Preheat oven to 375 degrees. Grease 2 twelve-cup mini-muffin tins, or 2 regular-sized 6-cup muffin tins. Combine flour, sugar, walnuts, lemon zest, salt, soda, baking powder, cinnamon, allspice, and cloves in a mixing bowl.

Combine eggs, vegetable oil, and vanilla in a separate bowl, and stir in the zucchini. Add the zucchini mixture to the dry ingredients, and stir until just combined.

Spoon into the prepared muffin tins. Bake for 12 to 15 minutes, or about 20 minutes for the larger muffins. When they are done, the muffins will be mounded in the center, and will be slightly springy to the touch.

Cool for 5 minutes in the pans, then remove to a rack. When they have cooled completely, store in a tightly sealed plastic bag. These muffins freeze well; in fact you can double this recipe, and make enough for lots of dinners.

SWEET ORANGE CHICKEN

Buy whole coriander and allspice, and crush them with the back of a spoon in a bowl, or with a mortar and pestle. Bake the chicken in a dish from which you can also serve it.

2 chicken quarters, washed, skin removed
1/2 cup orange juice
1/4 cup dry sherry
2 tablespoons brown sugar
1/4 teaspoon crushed coriander
1/4 teaspoon crushed allspice
Salt and freshly ground black pepper to taste

Preheat oven to 375 degrees. Place chicken quarters in a baking dish. Combine orange juice, sherry, brown sugar, coriander, allspice, salt, and pepper in a small bowl. Stir well, and pour over chicken. Bake uncovered for one hour, basting occasionally, until chicken is lightly browned, and no longer pink throughout. Serve with the cooking juices, which can be used as a light sauce or gravy.

RICE PILAF SERVED WITH GREEN BEANS

Pilaf is a rice cooked with vegetables. This one is a nice accompaniment to chicken.

1 cup Basmati rice
(or another extra-long grain white rice)
2 cups water
1 tablespoon butter
2 green onions, green part included, chopped
1/2 cup sliced white button mushrooms
1/4 cup chopped carrots
2 tablespoons chopped fresh parsley
1 teaspoon salt
about 4 ounces fresh green beans,
(washed and trimmed, but otherwise left whole)

Measure the rice into a saucepan, and pour the water over it. Set it on the stove over medium heat. Add the butter, green onions, mushrooms, carrots, parsley, and salt. Cover, bring to a boil, reduce the heat to low, and cook until all the water is absorbed, about 20 minutes.

Meanwhile, cook the green beans until crisp-tender and bright green, about 3 minutes in a microwave, or 5 minutes steamed. Serve on a plate with the rice pilaf.

BAKED APPLES

Warm baked apples make a perfect ending to a fall supper.

2 large, perfect, baking apples;
(use McIntosh, Jonathan, Cortland, or Granny Smith)
Juice of 1/2 lemon
1/4 cup chopped almonds
2 tablespoons brown sugar
1/2 teaspoon cinnamon
1 tablespoon grated lemon zest
1 tablespoon sweet red wine,
or sweet German Auslese
(optional) 1/2 cup whipping cream

Preheat oven to 375 degrees. Lightly grease a baking dish. Cut the tops off the apples, and cut out the core, but don't cut all the way through. Squeeze the lemon juice into a small bowl, dip the cut tops of the apples in it, and place the apples in the baking dish. Combine the almonds, brown sugar, cinnamon, lemon zest, and red wine in a small bowl. Stuff the resulting paste into the apples. Add a splash of water to the lemon juice in the small bowl, and pour it into the bottom of the baking dish. Bake for about an hour, until the apples are soft but still retain their shape. Serve warm, with whipping cream (which could be loosely whipped with 1 tablespoon sugar and 1 teaspoon vanilla), if desired.

SERVING YOUR ROMANTIC HARVEST

Tuck a few real fall leaves of different colors into each napkin.

Serve the steamed scallops in shallow stoneware bowls. Enjoy your cocktail or dry white wine with them.

Move on to your soup course; spoon the carrot soup into soup bowls. Pile the muffins into a basket lined with a napkin. They are great with the soup, but leave them on the table to eat with the entrée, too.

Serve the chicken in its baking dish (a shallow, uncovered, handmade, pottery baker would be perfect), with its juices, and a big spoon with which to spoon it out. Serve the rice and green beans from the kitchen, leaving room on the plates for the chicken. Pour your reisling into stemmed glasses.

If you baked the apples in another shallow, uncovered, handmade, pottery baker, serve them from it, into small bowls which will accommodate the cream, which you can serve in a small pitcher. Pour your coffee into cups that match your dinner plates, and your sweet Auslese wine into stemmed wine glasses.

Chapter 16

WARM MY HEART

Bruschetta

Spinach Salad

Carrot Pecan Bread

Rack of Lamb
Served with Parsley Buttered Potatoes

Chocolate Cheesecake

Old Fashioned Cocktail (see recipe, page 62)
or Chardonnay

Cabernet Sauvignon

Coffee or Cappuccino and
Late Harvest Zinfandel or Port

*T*his is a rich and luxurious menu, sensuous with flavors, textures, and colors. Serve it on elegant china, with a jewel-toned quilt or scarf for a table cloth, white damask napkins, and three or four votive candles in crystal holders at each place. If it is late enough in the fall to get winterberry, arrange a few branches in a large vase. Otherwise, arrange a combination of gourds, Indian corn, and various dried weeds.

INGREDIENTS AND PLANNING

Check each recipe; make a list of the ingredients you don't have on hand. Check your liquor cabinet and wine cellar. Don't forget a stop at the liquor store if necessary.

Buy the basil for your bruschetta, and the spinach for your salad, as well as any of the other vegetables (tomato, green pepper, zucchini, scallions, red onion, mushrooms, carrots, new potatoes, and parsley) that aren't already in your refrigerator.

Unless you have a homemade French baguette in your freezer (in which case you should take it out to thaw), buy one at a bakery.

Unless you are sure your butcher stocks it, call ahead to order a rack of lamb. Ask for a small one — one to one and a half pounds, two pounds at the absolute maximum. Ask that the bones be left long, and that the fat be trimmed very carefully.

If you find the prospect of making your own chocolate cheesecake with a chocolate sponge cake base a bit daunting, don't hesitate to stop in at your favorite bakery or delicatessen for the professionally made version.

Weeds are weeds in the summer, but by late autumn, when they are dry and brown, they take on a new life indoors. An expedition to the countryside, or to the back of a little-used parking lot, to gather some interesting specimens can be fun for the whole family. Dried weeds can be spray-painted any color, including white or metallic gold, which makes a great Christmas and winter decorating tool. If you don't have time to gather them yourself, craft stores are frequently a good source of dried weeds. Buy winterberry from a florist. Put it in water, and it will last for about six weeks.

When you plan your music for the evening, think of the dark evenings, bare tree branches, and eery sense of change in late fall. It makes us think of the eery sounds of Andreas Vollenweider, especially the *Caverna Magica* album.

TO DO AHEAD

Cheesecake really should be made a day ahead, or even two or three days ahead, so it can properly chill and set. If your only time to cook during the week is in the evenings, you could make the chocolate sponge cake base one evening, and the cheesecake filling the next. And, here is a little known cheesecake fact: though many doyens in the field would blanch at the thought, the truth is that cheesecake can be frozen. You can freeze it whole, while it is still in the pan, or remove it from the pan, and cut it into quarters. In any case, wrap it tightly, and use it within two months. Thaw overnight in the refrigerator.

If today is the day of your romantic dinner, you haven't made your cheesecake ahead, and you don't want to buy it, make it first thing in the morning, so it can chill as long as possible. It will take up oven space for at least three hours, but luckily the rest of the baking can wait.

Make the carrot bread next, and roast a head of garlic for the bruschetta. You can also mix the vegetables for the bruschetta; put them in a small covered bowl, and refrigerate until you need them.

Be innovative with your tablecloth tonight; use a silk scarf, an old quilt, or anything else you can find with deep, jewel colors. If the cloth is thin, pad the table with a blanket or towel. Make sure your best white damask napkins are pressed and ready.

Make an arrangement of dried weeds and gourds, or winterberry, for your table.

Next, make the mustard sauce for the rack of lamb, and spread it on about half an hour before you plan to cook it. Wash, dry, and tear up the spinach leaves for salad, and mix the dressing in the bottom of the salad bowl.

TASKS FOR CHILDREN

Making cheesecake amounts to one long and intimate session with your electric mixer. If you want to enlist your preschooler's help, set a stable chair securely by the counter next to the mixer, and give instructions in how to scrape the sides of the bowl without getting the scraper caught in the beaters. Other preschooler tasks include piling chopped vegetables onto French bread slices and sprinkling with mozzarella cheese for the Bruschetta, and serving as food processor operator during the grating of carrots for carrot bread.

A six to nine year old could be of a bit more help with the cheesecake, especially one interested in egg separating practice. One could measure and mix ingredients for the carrot bread, chop the pecans, make garlic butter, chop vegetables, slice bread, and grate cheese for bruschetta, and spread mustard sauce on the rack of lamb. One could set the table, unless you don't want to miss the pleasure of setting a special table for your true love.

A nine to twelve year old might be ready to take on cheesecake, with you as a fairly active assistant. Teach the technique of folding in stiffly beaten egg whites without crushing them, point out how the color and texture of batter changes with prolonged beating, and hand over the responsibility of timing the various stages of baking and cooling. He or she could certainly be completely in charge of carrot bread, spinach salad, mustard sauce for the lamb, and parsley buttered potatoes.

SHARING THE WORK

At the appropriate time,

COOK A	COOK B
assembles bruschetta	serves cocktails or wine
broils bruschetta	assembles salad
puts lamb in the oven	starts cooking potatoes
(luckily, lamb bakes at a temperature very close to broiling)	
	warms bread
pours wine	serves bread and salad
serves entrée	
makes coffee	clears table
pours wine	serves dessert

BRUSCHETTA

Bruschetta is a tomato, basil, and mozzarella cheese canape, broiled just long enough to warm the vegetables and melt the cheese. You can use homemade French bread, if you happen to have some on hand, or purchased French bread. We spread ours with the same garlic butter we used on the garlic bread in Chapter Ten.

2 tablespoons roasted garlic (*instructions below*)
2 tablespoons softened butter
1 small tomato, chopped
1/4 of a small green bell pepper, chopped
2-inch section of a small zucchini, chopped
2 green onions, green part included, chopped
1/4 cup chopped, loosely packed fresh basil,
6 to 10 slices French bread,
sliced diagonally for maximum diameter
1 cup shredded mozzarella cheese

To roast the garlic, place a whole, unpealed head in a pie pan, and roast at 350 degrees for one hour. Let it cool until it can be handled. Gently peal off the outer cloves, and scrape out the contents with a butter knife, until you have the amount you need. Combine it with the softened butter.

Leave the rest of the garlic head intact, and store it in a tightly sealed plastic bag in the refrigerator. Use it whenever you have a need for crushed garlic.

Preheat broiler. Combine the tomato, green bell pepper, zucchini, green onions, and basil in a small bowl. Spread the bread slices with garlic butter, pile on the vegetable mixture, and top with the cheese. Broil for 3 minutes, until the cheese melts and browns slightly. Serve warm.

SPINACH SALAD

This is a tangy dressing for fresh spinach. If you like, you can toss about 1 tablespoon crisply cooked, crumbled bacon into the finished salad.

1 clove garlic, crushed
1/4 teaspoon Dijon style mustard
Salt and freshly ground black pepper to taste
1 tablespoon lemon juice
3 tablespoons extra virgin olive oil
1 pound raw spinach, stems removed,
(*leaves carefully washed, dried, and torn*)
4 thin slices red onion, separated into rings
1/2 cup sliced white button mushrooms

Combine the garlic, mustard, salt, and pepper in the bottom of a wooden salad bowl. Mix lemon juice and olive oil, and add to the bowl. Add spinach, onion, and mushrooms, toss well. Serve at once.

CARROT PECAN BREAD

This bread is also delicious spread with softened cream cheese as an hors d'oeuvre.

1/3 cup vegetable oil
1/2 cup packed brown sugar
1 tablespoon grated orange zest
1 egg, lightly beaten
1/4 cup milk
1 cup flour
1/2 teaspoon baking powder
1/2 teaspoon salt
1/2 teaspoon ground allspice
1/4 teaspoon baking soda
2 cups loosely packed grated carrots
1/2 cup chopped pecans

Preheat oven to 350 degrees. Grease two 3x6x2-inch loaf pans.

Cream oil, sugar, and orange zest. Add egg and milk; continue beating until fluffy. Combine flour, baking powder, baking soda, salt, and allspice in a small bowl. Add to sugar mixture, and continue beating until smooth. Fold in carrots and pecans.

Divide batter equally between the two loaf pans. Bake for 30 to 40 minutes, until the loaves begin to pull away from the sides of the pan, and a toothpick inserted in center comes out clean.

Cool on a rack for about 10 minutes, remove from pans, and cool for another 20 minutes before slicing. Store in a tightly sealed plastic bag. An uncut loaf can be frozen. Let it thaw completely at room temperature before slicing.

RACK OF LAMB SERVED WITH
PARSLEY BUTTERED POTATOES

A very small rack of lamb makes an elegant dinner for two, especially if the bones are left long and graceful.

2 tablespoons honey mustard
2 cloves garlic, chopped fine
2 teaspoons chives or 2 green onions,
  green parts included, chopped fine
2 tablespoons olive oil
salt and freshly ground pepper to taste
a 1 to 1-1/2 pound rack of lamb
4 new potatoes, scrubbed and cut in half,
  or 1 large potato, peeled and cut into 8 pieces
1 tablespoon butter
1 tablespoon parsley, chopped

Preheat oven to 450 degrees. Place the rack of lamb on a broiler pan, fat side up. Mix the mustard, garlic, chives, olive oil, and salt and pepper into a paste. Coat the top of the rack of lamb with the paste. Bake for 25 minutes, until well browned outside, but rare inside. Meanwhile, cook the potatoes in water to cover for about 15 minutes, until tender. Drain. Add butter and parsley to the pan, and mix. To serve, slice the rack of lamb between the bones, and put two slices, bones crossed, on each dinner plate, with the potatoes.

CHOCOLATE CHEESECAKE

Many otherwise rational people have very strong feelings about cheesecake. This recipe reflects our position on the subject; we are firmly in the dense, heavy, rich, to-die-for camp. We also subscribe to the cheesecake theory which says that the best ones don't come in crumb crusts, but instead are massive toppings for thin layers of sponge cake. This admittedly turns it into quite a baking project. If you are of the crumb crust school, make one for this cake by combining 2-1/4 cups chocolate wafer crumbs with 1/2 cup melted butter; press the mixture into the bottom of a buttered 10-inch springform pan.

Chocolate sponge cake base:

3 tablespoons flour

2 tablespoons unsweetened cocoa powder

3 eggs

1/2 cup sugar

1 teaspoon vanilla

Preheat oven to 425 degrees. Generously butter the bottom and sides of a 10-inch springform pan. Sift the flour and cocoa together 3 times. Separate 2 of the eggs. Set aside the egg whites, and add the yolks to the whole egg, broken into a mixing bowl. Add the sugar and vanilla to the egg yolk mixture. Beat with an electric mixer on high for 5 minutes, until light, fluffy, and increased in volume. Add half of the flour-cocoa mixture, beat until completely absorbed, and then add the rest. Continue beating for another five minutes.

Beat the egg whites separately until very stiff. Fold into the chocolate mixture. Pour the batter into the prepared pan, smoothing it with a spatula. Place the springform pan on a baking sheet, in case some of the batter leaks out during baking. Bake for 8 to 10 minutes, until a toothpick inserted in center comes out clean, and the sponge cake feels springy to the touch.

Cool on a rack. As it cools, the sponge cake will shrink in height, and pull slightly away from the sides of the pan. It may still look a little high to serve as a cheesecake base, but when you load on almost 3 pounds of filling, it will flatten out nicely.

Chocolate cheesecake filling:

12 ounces semi-sweet chocolate chips

2 (8 ounce) packages cream cheese

1 teaspoon vanilla

1/4 teaspoon salt

1 cup sugar

1 egg

4 egg yolks

1 (16 ounce) container sour cream

Preheat oven to 325 degrees. In small bowl or double boiler melt the chocolate over gently boiling water. Remove from heat, and stir until smooth. Set aside to cool. Beat cream cheese with vanilla, salt, and sugar until very smooth. Add egg, beat well again. Add each egg yolk separately, beat well after each addition. Add chocolate, beat until completely combined. Add the sour cream in two additions, beating well after each.

Pour the batter into the springform pan containing the chocolate sponge cake base (or the chocolate wafer crumb crust, if you made that), and set the pan on a baking sheet, in case some of the batter leaks out during baking. Bake for 1 hour. Turn off the oven, but don't open the door, and leave the cake in for another hour. Open the oven door, and leave the cake in for another 30 minutes. Remove to a rack, and cool for another hour. Cover tightly with aluminum foil, and chill overnight — or at least for several hours, as long as you can restrain yourself from cutting into it. Remove from the pan by sliding a sharp knife around the edge, loosening the spring mechanism on the side of the pan, and lifting off the ring. Cut it and serve it cold, in small portions. If you like, you can dress it up and add some color with a few berries, curls of lemon zest, or slivers cut from a bar of white chocolate. This cake could serve up to sixteen people for a dinner party or buffet.

SERVING YOUR LATE AUTUMN FEAST

Scatter a few gourds and pine cones among the candles on your table.

Arrange the bruschetta in a single layer on a tray, on a large serving platter, or in a large flat basket. Enjoy it with your Old Fashioned or Chardonnay.

Slice one loaf of your carrot bread and arrange it in a small basket lined with a napkin. Put a plate of softened butter, and a butter spreader, on the table. Serve your spinach salad from the kitchen, on fine china or clear glass salad plates.

You can carve the rack of lamb at the table, if you have an elegant little cutting board with a well to catch the juices. Otherwise, carve it in the kitchen, though you will probably want seconds. Serve it on a dinner plate, with the potatoes. Pour the Cabernet Sauvignon into stemmed crystal glasses.

If your cheesecake has had a full day to chill, take it out of the refrigerator at the beginning of your meal. Otherwise, leave it in until the last minute. What else can we say about cheesecake? Serve it on fine china dessert plates, with your cappuccino and dessert wine, and enjoy the sensation that you've died and gone to heaven.

RECIPE INDEX

GENERAL INDEX

A

Active Listening, 55
Ahead, To Do, 79, 89, 99, 109, 118, 127, 135, 144
Alsatian Wine, 66, 107, 115
Ambiance, 21, 26
Asparagus Spears and Grilled Salmon Filets, 107
Asti Spumanti, 66, 97, 106
Auslese, 66, 67, 107, 115, 134, 142

B

Babies, 45, 46
Baked Apples, 67, 134
Balsamic Vinaigrette Dressing, 97
Barware, 61-62
Beaujolais, 65, 66, 78, 87
Beer, 72, 125, 133
Berries, Frozen, 23
Blanc de Noirs, 65, 88, 96
Blueberry Muffins, 116
Bourbon, 62
and Soda, 62, 134, 142
Brandy, 65, 67, 70, 125, 133
Brandy, French Napoleon, 67
Bread, Carrot Pecan, 143
Bread, Cracker, 97
Bread, French, 78
Bread, Garlic, 88
Bread, Italian Herb (Focaccia), 97
Bread Sticks, Rosemary, 125
Bruschetta, 70, 143
Burgundy, White, 66, 97, 106

C

Cabernet Sauvignon, 67, 143, 151
Caesar Salad, 65, 78
as a dinner, 70
Cake, Whidbey's Pound, 69-70, 78
Calamari, Crispy, 65, 70, 78
Carrot Pecan Bread, 143
Carrots and Summer Squash, Julienned, 116
Carrot Soup, 70, 134
Chambord, 66, 116, 124
Champagne, 65
Chardonnay, 66, 67, 97, 106, 116, 143, 151
Cheese, Brie, 66, 97
Cheese, Dessert, 66, 107
Cheesecake, Chocolate, 67, 143
Cherry Tomatoes, Skewered, and Cucumbers with Avocado Slices, 116
Cherry Tomatoes, Herb Stuffed Mushrooms and, 88
Chicken Breast, Marinated, 116
Chicken, Sweet Orange, 134
Children
ages nine to twelve, 34-35, 50-51, 81, 91, 100, 110, 119, 128, 136, 146
ages six to nine, 34, 49-50, 81, 91, 100, 109, 119, 128, 136, 145
ages three to six, 33, 47-49, 80, 91, 100, 109, 118, 128, 136, 145
babies, 45, 46
cooking, 31
favorite foods, 37
helping, 27
meals, 36, 40-43
music, 50
needs, 11-12
planning their day, 20

Liqueur, Whidbey's, 65, 78, 87
Long Island Iced Tea, 63, 116, 124

M

Macaroni and Cheese with
   Hamburgers on Buns, 41-42
Mai Tai, 63
Manhattan, 62, 78, 87
Marinated Chicken Breasts, 116
Martini, 63, 97, 106
Massage, 76-77
Mint Julep, 71
Moderation, 60-61
Muffins, Blueberry, 116
Muffins, Tiny Zucchini, 134
Muscadet, 66, 125, 129, 133
Mushrooms, Herb Stuffed, and
   Cherry Tomatoes, 88
Mushrooms, wild, 23
Music, 21, 25-26, 79, 89, 98-99,
   108, 118, 127, 135, 144
   children's, 50
   playing together, 74
Mussels Steamed in White Wine, 125

N

Nuts, 23

O

Old Fashioned Cocktail, 62, 143,
   151
Open Ended Questions, 54-55

P

Parsley Buttered Potatoes, 143
Pasta Salad, 66, 116
Pasta, see Linguini, 97
Pilaf, Rice, 134
Pinot Grigio, 67, 134
Pinot Noir, 66, 107, 115

Pinot Noir, Willamet Valley, 66, 107
Planning, 16, 18, 79, 89, 98, 108,
   117, 126, 135, 144
   children's meals, 36
Poppy Seed Dressing, 107
Port, 67, 143
Potatoes, New, 125
Potatoes, Parsley Buttered, 143
Pound Cake, Whidbey's, 69-70, 78
Preschoolers, See Children, ages
   three to six

Q

Questions, Open Ended, 54-55

R

Rack of Lamb, 67, 143
Radicchio Salad with Honey Mustard
   Dressing, 88
Reading, 75
Reisling, German, 66, 97, 106
Reisling, Spätlese, 67, 134
Rice, Lemon, 107
Rice, Pilaf, 134
Rice, Wild, 23
Rolls, Whole Wheat, 107
Rosemary Bread Sticks, 125
Routine, 45-47
Rum, 63

S

Safety, Kitchen, 32-33
Salad, Caesar, 65, 78
   as a dinner, 70
Salad, Garden-grown Tomato and
   Fresh Basil, 125
Salad, Green with Balsamic
   Vinaigrette Dressing, 97
Salad, Green with Strawberries and
   Poppy Seed Dressing, 107

ABOUT THE AUTHORS

Nan Booth and Gary Fischler, experienced as spouses and parents, attribute the success of their marriage to, among other things, the pleasure they have always taken in cooking and eating together.

Nan is a freelance writer and psychotherapist. She has Master's Degrees in both Social Work and Public Health, with a specialty in Maternal and Child Health, and has worked extensively on issues of relationship, family, and parenthood. Gary is a Clinical Psychologist. His Doctoral research and writing was on the subject of problem solving in families with small children.

They live in Minneapolis, Minnesota with their two sons, who take great pride in having learned how to make macaroni and cheese.